HO JAYEGA

Where Everything Is Urgent and Nothing Is Planned

ARUP NAG

Clever Fox PUBLISHING
Chennai • Bangalore

CLEVER FOX PUBLISHING
Chennai, India

Published by CLEVER FOX PUBLISHING 2026

ISBN: 978-93-7500-272-7

Disclaimer

This book is based on my experiences navigating Indian workplaces over three decades. Names have been changed, timelines compressed, and conversations recreated from memory.

Nobody remembers exact words from years ago.

This is not a management book. No advice. No frameworks. No success formulas.

Just stories. Honest, messy, sometimes funny, sometimes uncomfortable. About what actually happens at work in India.

If you recognise yourself in these pages, it's not personal.

We've all lived some version of this.

The details change. The chaos doesn't

For everyone who's ever said "ho jayega" without knowing how. And still showed up the next day.

ACKNOWLEDGMENTS

To every employee who got laid off on a Friday and job-hunted on Monday: you're tougher than you think.

To the managers who taught me what NOT to do - thank you for the material.

To the few managers who actually had my back - you know who you are.

To chai tapris everywhere, the real conference rooms of India.

A NOTE ON LANGUAGE

This book moves between English, Hindi, and Hinglish. Some phrases are left untranslated because their meaning lives in how they're said, not just what they mean.

CONTENTS

A MESSY CAREER MAP

This book doesn't move in a straight line.
It jumps around like Mumbai traffic. Here's the map:

Hotels | Kolkata
Five-star hotels, fine dining, nightclubs

Telecom | Kolkata
CAF forms, CDMA chaos, Salman Khan crisis

Retail Chain | Everywhere
Kolkata, Hyderabad, Bengaluru, Punjab, Jaipur, New Delhi
Thirteen years. Store openings, people chaos, festival madness, pink slips

Fashion Startup | Kolkata
Big ambitions. Bad timing. COVID.

Jaipur Startup | Post-COVID
Rebuilding. Again.

Multiple cities | Present
Still figuring it out. Still showing up.

Roles jumped around too.
Operations. Sales. Training. People.
Whatever needed doing.

The stories don't appear in this order.
They show up when they feel like it.

INTRODUCTION

Deadlines. Family calls. A boss pinging "where's the report?"

All at once. All urgent. All normal.

Welcome to work in India.

My career has zigzagged through hotels, telecom, retail, and consulting. Thirty years. No straight lines. No five-year plans that survived five months.

Diwali sale disasters. People who said "ho Jayega" right up to launch week. Employees with eight dead grandparents in one year.

Nothing unusual. That was work.

This isn't a career guide. I'm not a CEO. No corner office. No startup exit. No lessons on "winning at life."

Just workplace stories. The chaos. The politics. The quiet absurdity. And the humour you develop when the alternative is losing your mind.

Everything in this book happened. Names are changed. Timelines compressed. Conversations reconstructed from memory.

The absurdity, unfortunately, is intact.

If some of this feels unbelievable, that's fine. It felt the same while it was happening.

PART ONE

THE CIRCUS BEGINS

CHAPTER 1: The Indian Workplace Circus

The Salman Khan Bathroom Crisis

The Guy Who Said "Ho Jayega"

"May I Light You?"

The VIP, the Scotch, and the Bucket

From Job to Just Married

Talktime Unlimited

The Coffee That Spilled (And Somehow That Was Good Luck)

The Day We Invented an Accident

Balls for Breakfast

The Zoo Manager

VIPs Who Served the Floor

The Chicken Roll That Won Employee Loyalty (Accidentally)

CHAPTER 1

THE INDIAN WORKPLACE CIRCUS

The Salman Khan Bathroom Crisis

11:30 AM. Peak hour at the telecom counter.

Forty customers in queue. Four of us managing the chaos.

One of my team members, Priya, suddenly went pale.

"Sir, I need to use the restroom."

"Okay. Go."

She left. She didn't come back.

Fifteen minutes passed. We were down to three people on the floor.

I asked the other staff member, Rakesh, "Where's Priya?"

He shrugged. "Washroom, sir."

"For fifteen minutes?"

"Maybe stomach problem?"

Twenty minutes. Still no Priya. The queue was growing. Customers were getting louder.

I knocked on the women's washroom door.

"Priya? You okay?"

A muffled sound. Possibly crying.

"Priya, what's wrong?"

Her voice was shaky. "Sir, I can't come out."

"Why? Are you sick?"

"No, sir."

"Are you hurt? Do you need a doctor?"

"No, sir."

"Then what's going on?"

A long pause. Then:

"Salman Khan ko arrest kar liya."

I stared at the door. "What?"

"Salman Khan. They arrested him this morning. I got the news. I can't stop crying."

For a moment, I genuinely thought I'd misheard.

Outside, forty customers waiting.

Inside, one employee paralysed by Bollywood news.

I took a breath. "Priya, I understand you're upset. But we have customers … "

"I know, sir!" she cried. "But I can't stop crying. Every time I think about it, I start again!"

Rakesh came up behind me. "Sir, customers are complaining."

I looked at him. Looked at the bathroom door. Looked at the queue.

"Rakesh, handle the counter. I'll deal with this."

I stood outside the washroom for another ten minutes, talking Priya through it.

Not about work. About Salman Khan.

How he'd probably get bail.

How this wasn't the end of the world.

Finally, she came out. Eyes red. Face puffy.

"I'm sorry, sir."

"It's okay," I said. "Wash your face. Take five minutes. Then come back to the counter."

She did.

We survived the day. Barely.

That evening, my manager called.

"How was the day?"

"Interesting."

"Any issues?"

I almost told him about the Salman Khan crisis.

Then decided against it.

Some things are too absurd to explain.

The Guy Who Said "Ho Jayega"

Punjab store opening. Big launch. Whole city buzzing.

One department was assigned to a staff member. Mid-twenties. Permanently relaxed.

Every review meeting ended the same way.

"Stock sorted?"

"Ho jayega ji."

"Pricing done?"

"Ho jayega ji."

"Labels ready?"

"Ho jayega ji."

Same line. Same smile. Different day.

Two days before launch, I asked for a final walkthrough.

"Show me your section. Everything ready?"

He grinned. "Ho jayega ji."

"I want to see it. Now."

We walked onto the shop floor. I started checking. Shelf by shelf.

Empty spaces. Missing labels. Prices not marked. Stock sitting in boxes.

"This needs twenty units."

"Pricing pending here."

"Labels not done."

"That corner hasn't come yet."

The list kept growing.

I turned to him. "You've been saying 'ho jayega' for two weeks. Nothing's done."

He grinned again. "Galti ho gaya ji… ab kya, suli pe chadhaoge?"

Still not apologetic. Still relaxed.

"How long to fix all this?"

He thought for a moment. "Maybe… two days?"

"We have one."

His face changed. First time.

"Sir, I can't…"

"You should've thought of that during the last fifteen 'ho jayega's. Stop talking. Start working."

We worked till late night. I left at midnight. He stayed.

Next morning, 6 AM, I came back.

The section was ready. Shelves filled. Labels done. Prices marked.

He looked terrible. Red eyes. Crushed shirt.

"You finished?"

"Yes, sir. Just now."

"Go home. Sleep. Be back by 10."

Store opened. City showed up. Celebrity arrived. His section looked flawless.

* * *

Three months later, another store opening. Same guy.

I asked, "Ready?"

He didn't smile. Didn't say "ho jayega."

He said, "Yes, sir. I have a checklist."

"May I Light You?"

Hotel years. Coffee shop days. Cigarette smoking wasn't banned yet in hotels. We were very customer-service focused.

Boss instructed: "If you see anyone taking out a cigarette, offer to light it and carry your lighter." Fair point.

My manager was a chain smoker. Came for lunch, corner table reserved for him. Crowded that day.

New trainee sees him take out a cigarette. Either to impress him or nervous… maybe both… runs over with lighter.

Says: "May I light you?"

The manager looked at him. "What did you just say?"

He froze.

"I... I meant... may I light your cigarette, sir?"

The manager stared at him for what felt like five minutes. Then burst out laughing.

Half the coffee shop turned to stare.

The trainee looked mortified. Face red, hands shaking.

Manager waved him off. "It's fine. Just... think before you speak next time."

"Yes, sir. Sorry, sir."

The trainee practically ran back to the counter.

Later, the manager called me. "Your trainee just offered to set me on fire."

"I heard, sir."

"Train them properly. Next time someone might take offense."

"Yes, sir."

Summoned again.

But honestly, I couldn't be mad. It was too funny.

The trainee, let's call him Amit, was devastated. Thought he'd get fired.

"Sir, I'm so sorry. I don't know what I was thinking…."

"Relax. You're not fired. The manager laughed it off."

"Really?"

"Really. But next time, say 'May I light your cigarette' not 'May I light you.' Big difference."

He nodded, still looking embarrassed.

Two weeks later, same trainee saw a guest take out a cigarette. Walked over, lighter in hand, carefully said: "Sir, may I light your cigarette for you?"

Guest smiled. "Thank you."

Amit came back looking relieved. "Sir, I got it right this time."

"Good. Keep practicing."

He did. Became one of our best floor staff. Still tells the "may I light you" story at parties, apparently.

The VIP, the Scotch, and the Bucket

Room service guy. Old-timer. Two months from retirement. Sweet. Always on time.

But he had this twitch. Every few seconds, his head would jerk to one side. Sharp. Quick. After a week, you stopped noticing.

One afternoon, Front Office Manager calls.

"Boss, big problem. Guest is upset. VIP. Let's go."

We head up. Guest's in his room with two others. Business meeting. Drinks on the table.

Guest's polite but clearly annoyed.

"Gentlemen, I called room service for an ice bucket. Look what they sent."

He points.

An 18-year-old Scotch and three crystal glasses sat neatly on the side table.

Right below it, against the wall, was a bright blue plastic bucket.

I almost lost it.

"Sir, so sorry. This is completely unacceptable. We'll replace it immediately."

Sent a proper ice bucket. Sent snacks on the house. Apologized five more times. Somehow calmed him down.

Back at the pantry, I called the team.

"What happened?"

The old man looked nervous.

"Sir, guest asked for a bucket. We don't keep buckets in room service. So I called housekeeping. They sent one."

I stared at him.

"Why would a guest call room service for a bucket?"

One steward spoke up quietly.

"Sir, I think I know."

He explained.

Guest had called and said: "Can I get some snacks and an ice bucket?"

Right at the word ice, our man's head jerked.

Missed it completely.

He only heard: bucket.

So he did exactly what the guest asked for.

Got him a bucket.

Bright blue. Plastic. Fresh from housekeeping.

Delivered it to the VIP's room. Positioned it carefully. Left.

That's how a bucket ended up next to three confused businessmen and premium whiskey.

The old man felt terrible once he understood.

"Sir, I didn't hear properly. So sorry."

We couldn't be mad. Guy was two months from retirement. Had worked twenty years without a single major complaint.

Guest checked out the next day.

Left a note: "Service was... memorable."

From Job to Just Married

Two employees stopped showing up. No calls. Phones switched off.

Day one: sick, probably. Day two: phones still off. I called emergency contacts, parents in remote villages, no mobiles.

Day three: absconding letters issued.

Then the families called. Panicking.

"Our son hasn't come home. We don't know where he is. Have you seen him?"

"Our daughter didn't come back from work three days ago. Where is she?"

Now I'm panicking. Two employees missing. Both families clueless.

I filed missing persons reports. Police involved. This was serious.

Two days later…almost a week now…both of them walked into the store. Smiling. Holding hands.

HR went from relieved to furious in two seconds.

"Where the hell have you been? Your families are worried sick! We filed police reports!"

The guy, totally calm: "We ran away and got married."

Silence.

"You... what?"

"We're in love. Our parents wouldn't approve. So we eloped. Got married. We're husband and wife now."

The girl, nodding: "We didn't have money for a proper honeymoon, so we're back. Can we rejoin work?"

I'm standing there thinking, you disappeared for a week, caused a police investigation, and now you're asking to just... come back?

HR: "You can't just disappear without informing anyone! Your families thought you were kidnapped!"

Guy: "But we're married now. It's all fine."

It wasn't fine. Their families were furious, not because they got married, but because they vanished without a word. HR was furious because we'd wasted time and resources on a police case that turned out to be a love story.

They were both let go. Absconding.

Policy did what policy does.

The police closed the case. "Waste of resources," they said.

The couple left, still holding hands, probably thinking we were the unreasonable ones.

Talktime Unlimited

Telecom days. Tata Walky. Fixed wireless phones. Fixed locations. Fixed assumptions.

One afternoon, a furious father walked into our service centre clutching a bill.

"This is fraud. You are cheating customers."

The bill was massive. Shockingly massive, for a phone that, according to him, was barely used.

"Sir, let's check the call details."

He folded his arms confidently. "I sleep by ten. Phone is near me. No one touches it. How can this much usage happen?"

Backend team pulled out the call logs.

Long calls. Late nights. Hours together. Every single night.

We double-checked. Everything was clean. No system error. No billing fraud.

"Sir, are there other family members at home?"

He nodded. "My daughter. Very decent girl. Studies hard. Sleeps early."

I showed him the logs. Calls starting at 10:15 PM. Ending at 2 AM. Every night. For weeks.

His face went through several expressions.

Confusion.

Realization.

Disbelief.

Anger.

Then silence.

He folded the bill carefully. Cleared his throat.

"Cancel the connection."

"Sir, are you sure? If you want, we can set usage limits, block late-night …"

"Cancel it."

He walked out.

We didn't lose a customer that day. Just cancelled the connection.

He went home with the bill. Probably had a conversation with his "very decent daughter."

And somewhere, a love story ended because the billing system was accurate.

True love doesn't care about phone bills.

Unfortunately, phone bills care about true love.

The Coffee That Spilled (And Somehow That Was Good Luck)

Saturday night. Coffee shop packed. Food festival week.

Every table full. Line waiting.

Limited staff. Trainees doing everything.

F&B manager on the floor. Stress high.

One mistake and he'll notice.

Table near the desk. Six guests. Foreigners. Ordered six different coffees.

Café Macchiato. Café Mocha. Cioccolino. Some Italian tongue-twister I can barely pronounce.

New steward serving. Young guy, nervous. First week on floor.

He's carrying the tray. Six cups. Balancing carefully.

Gets to the table. Starts placing cups down.

First cup. Fine.

Second. Good.

Third. Okay.

Fourth …

His hand slips.

Last cup tips. Coffee spills. All over the guest.

Silence.

The entire table goes quiet.

F&B manager's staring at me from across the room.

I'm staring at the steward.

Trainee's frozen. Tray still in hand. Face pale.

My brain's racing:

Guest's going to explode.

F&B manager's going to murder me.

Complimentary dinner.

Free dessert.

Discount voucher.

Shit.

All in two seconds.

I rush over. “Sir, I’m so sorry …”

The guest looks up. Smiling.

Wait. Smiling?

“It’s okay! Don’t worry!”

His friends at the table are laughing. Not angry laughing. Just... laughing.

“Really, it’s fine. Happens!”

I’m confused. “Sir, your shirt…”

“It’ll dry. No problem.”

The steward’s stammering apologies. “Sir, so sorry, sir, I didn’t mean…”

Guest waves him off. “Relax. It’s just coffee.”

We get him fresh napkins. Offer a new cup. Complimentary.

He accepts. Still smiling.

After things calm down, I go back to chat.

“Sir, thank you for being so understanding. Most guests would’ve been upset.”

He laughs. “In our country, spilling coffee is good luck.”

I blink. "What?"

"Yeah. Old belief. Spilled coffee means good fortune coming."

His friend chimes in: "Better than spilling wine. That's bad luck."

They're all grinning.

I wanted to hug them.

F&B manager walks by.

Glances at the table. Looks at me. "Everything okay?"

"Yes, sir. All handled."

He nods. Moves on.

Crisis averted.

Not because I did something brilliant.

But because the guests were chill.

Later, the steward came up to me. "Sir, I thought I was going to get fired."

"You're fine. Just be more careful."

"Those guests were so nice."

"Yeah. We got lucky."

"Sir, you think it's true? Spilling coffee is good luck?"

I looked at him. "For you? Today it was."

The steward didn't spill another cup for the rest of his time with us.

Maybe the good luck worked.

The Day We Invented an Accident

Peak hours in Room Service. Every guest in the hotel decided to order food at the same time.

Phones ringing.

Kitchen drowning.

Staff missing.

Orders delayed.

Irritated guest called: “Why is it taking so long?”

Standard line: “It’s on the way.”

Five minutes later, same guest, angrier.

We had nothing ready. No staff free. No fresh excuse left.

The order taker is flustered.

That’s when my captain calmly says:

“Tell him there was a small accident.”

I stare at him.

He continues as if narrating a weather report:

“Say the service lift stopped working… so the boy was walking up the stairs… he slipped a little… fell… and the kitchen had to remake the order.”

A full scripted accident…rehearsed in five seconds.

The order taker called the guest and repeated it.

Silence.

Then the guest's tone instantly changed:

"Oh… I hope he's okay."

"No problem… take your time."

"Please tell him to be careful."

Order was still nowhere near ready.

But the anger had evaporated completely.

In hospitality, a believable excuse works faster than the actual food.

Balls for Breakfast

Telecom days. Morning briefing. Manager pacing, stressed about some deadline.

Twenty of us sitting there. Standard manager stress speech.

Then he stopped. Centre of the room. Looked at us.

"If this doesn't happen on time…"

Long pause.

"…I will have your balls for breakfast."

Room went silent.

Nobody laughed. Nobody moved.

He stood there. Arms crossed. Waiting for us to absorb the threat.

Next day. Deadline day.

Morning comes. We're waiting for the CAF verification report. His team was supposed to finish the last batch the night before.

Nothing came.

Ten o'clock. Still nothing.

Eleven o'clock. Regional office calls.

"Where's the report?"

Turns out, half the CAFs weren't even checked. The team had gone home at 10 PM.

Deadline missed. Regional office furious.

That afternoon, he's sitting at his desk looking miserable.

I walked over. Leaned in. Kept my voice low.

"Looks like you missed the delicious breakfast, sir."

He froze. Looked up.

For a second I thought I'd crossed a line.

Then he laughed. "Fair point."

Never heard him make dramatic threats again.

The Zoo Manager

Back in hotel days, I was managing a coffee shop. Young team. Fresh hospitality management graduates. Most from the same college, good bonding.

They had nicknames.

Cheetah for his speed.

Unth (camel) for his height.

My manager was a terror. Called early mornings to check the situation.

One day, a trainee picked up. Landline.

Trainee: "Good morning, how may I help you?"

"Yes, what is the staff position?"

"Sir, we have Cheetah in one side station and Unth in the other, and I am handling the desk."

The manager came to office, called the desk:

"Send the manager of the zoo to my office."

The guy who received the call was confused. He told me, "Boss said this... I think he is calling you to his chamber!"

Till then I had no clue what had happened.

I entered and got blasted.

"What kind of names are these? Cheetah? Unth? This is a five-star hotel, not a zoo!"

"Sir, they're just nicknames the trainees use among themselves…"

"I don't care what they use among themselves! When I call and ask for staff position, I expect proper names. Not animal names!"

"Yes, sir."

"Tell your team: no more nicknames on official calls. If I hear 'Cheetah' or 'Unth' again, I'm putting this on record for the whole team."

"Yes, sir."

I left his office trying not to laugh.

Back at the coffee shop, I gathered the team.

"Next time the manager calls, use real names.

No Cheetah. No Unth."

They looked at me for a second.

Then started laughing.

Unth, actual name Rajeev said,

"Sir… did he really say zoo?"

"He did."

That set them off again.

Twenty years later, I called a 5-star caterer for a catering requirement. Manager picked up.

"I am Rajeev. I was with you in that coffee shop."

"Rajeev who?"

"Arey Sir…The Unth!"

We laughed.

Twenty years.

Still the Unth.

VIPs Who Served the Floor

I was handling a South East Asian cuisine restaurant.

Good food. Impeccable food. Not your safe hotel buffet. The kind of kitchen people remembered.

Hotel crews had one privilege…free meals.

Pilots. Cabin crew. Ground staff.

Show your badge, eat for free.

I made friends with a few of them. Real friendships. Not LinkedIn friendships.

And they figured out a hack.

Whenever they came in, they placed extra orders.

Serious extras.

Dishes marked for the crew.

Desserts for the crew. Drinks for the crew.

Officially, it was their food.

Unofficially, everyone knew where it would go.

The extra food wasn't for them alone.

It went to the floor staff.

The tired ones.

The permanently underpaid hospitality soldiers who still kept the floor moving.

Their arrival became a festival.

Work got faster. Smiles became real. Patience improved.

Stewards would wait for them. Not guests. Not VIPs.

Just those beautiful uniformed legends.

Then one day, they stopped coming.

Different routes. Different hotels. Different lives.

The free meals ended. The feasts ended.

Kitchen went back to normal. Work went back to quiet.

But the waiting stayed for a while.

I don't remember all the VIPs who ate there. Don't remember the reviews. Don't remember the complaints.

But I still remember the crew.

And how good food tastes when it's shared.

The Chicken Roll That Won Employee Loyalty (Accidentally)

Twenty years later, I ran into an ex-colleague from my hotel days.

She looked thrilled, emotional, borderline nostalgic, which immediately made me suspicious.

She said, "I will never forget what you did for me."

My brain panicked.

What had I done?

Was I rude? Did I forget to approve her leave in 1998? Did I scold her?

I braced for impact.

She said, "You saved my life once… with a chicken roll."

I said, "What?"

She explained.

Back then she worked in the business centre, young, overworked, doing the job of three people for the salary of half a person.

One particular mad day, she hadn't eaten.

I had casually asked, "Lunch ho gaya?"

She said she was swamped.

And apparently, I don't remember this at all…I'd sent someone to get her a chicken roll.

That roll became her lunch.

Her survival kit.

Her emotional support system.

And she remembered it two decades later.

All I could think was:

"One chicken roll and I became Mother Teresa?"

Hotels run on chaos.

But sometimes they also run on forgotten kindness… mostly forgotten by the person who actually did them.

Which makes me wonder:

how many other chicken rolls did I send without realising they mattered?

Chapter 2: There Was No Plan

From Sir to Salesman

The Security Guard Who Remembered

The Colleague Who Stole My CV

The Apology I Didn't Expect (And the One I Got)

CHAPTER 2

THERE WAS NO PLAN

From Sir to Salesman

After hotels, I joined a retail chain. Before the store opened, we had to build a customer base. Door-to-door. Offices, companies, hotels-didn't matter. Pitching a concept nobody had heard of.

"We're opening a cash-and-carry store. Wholesale prices. Membership based. Want to register?"

Half said, "Call me when it opens." Translation: I don't believe this is real.

The other half? Security guards shooed us away before we could get through the gate.

One day, outside a mid sized hotel, I tried to reach the purchase manager.

"No visitors without appointment," the guard said.

"I just need five minutes..."

"Move."

I froze. Back in hotels, I'd been running pubs and restaurants. Movie stars knew my name. VIPs asked for me. Guests shook my hand.

Now I couldn't even get past the gate. I felt invisible.

We kept going, different offices, different guards, same rejection. Some days, one person would register. Some days, nothing.

Eventually, the store opened. Huge success. And those same companies that wouldn't give us five minutes? They signed up immediately.

But I never forgot standing outside that gate. The security guard staring through me like I was air.

The Security Guard Who Remembered

Three months later, I got a call from a hotel purchase manager.

The address sounded familiar.

I reached the gate. Same hotel. Same guard.

He squinted at me.

"Aren't you that retail guy?"

"Yes. Here to meet the purchase manager."

He nodded. Gate opened. I walked in.

Inside, the manager was waiting. "Glad you came back," he said. "We should have signed up during your first visit."

We signed them up, regional membership, multiple properties.

I walked out. Glanced back.

The guard gave a small nod. No words. Just acknowledgement.

And that was it.

The Colleague Who Stole My CV

Early hotel days. About a year into my first job.

My colleague, let's call him Vikram, came to me one day.

"There's an opening at a competitor hotel. You should apply."

"Not interested. I just started here."

"But it's better property. Better pay."

"Maybe later."

He wouldn't let it go. Every few days: "Have you applied yet?"

"You're wasting time here." "That opening won't last forever."

"Vikram, if you're so interested, you apply."

"I already did. But you should too."

"I'm not ready."

"Okay." He dropped it. Or so I thought.

Two weeks later, I get a call. HR from the competitor hotel.

"We received your application. Can you come for an interview on Thursday?"

I'm confused. "I didn't apply."

"Your CV came through internal reference. Thursday, 3 PM. Can you make it?"

Then it hit me. Vikram.

I confronted him. "You went into my locker?"

"It wasn't locked. And you're welcome."

I wanted to be mad. But I was curious now.

Went for the interview. Thursday, 3 PM. Vikram went too.

A week later, I got the call. "We'd like to offer you the position."

Vikram? Nothing.

He was shocked. "How did you get it? You didn't even want to apply!"

"I didn't. You applied for me."

"But I'm the one who wanted it!"

"Maybe that's why they didn't pick you. Maybe, you seemed too desperate to them."

Vikram didn't talk to me for a week.

I took the job. Better property. Better team. Better growth.

And it only happened because someone broke into my locker.

The Apology I Didn't Expect (And the One I Got)

Part One

Retail days. Interview drive. Junior role. Hundreds of applicants.

One guy, maybe 23, 24, came through two rounds. Didn't make the cut.

I called him in. "We're not moving forward with your application."

He stared at me. "Why not?"

"Experience doesn't match what we need. Skills aren't aligned."

"But I was referred!"

"Being referred gets you an interview. Doesn't guarantee selection."

He got loud. Defensive. "I deserve this job. You're making a mistake."

I stayed calm. Explained again. Same answer.

He stormed out.

Next day, he came back. More agitated. Walked straight to my cabin.

"I want my resume back."

We kept resumes on file. Company policy. But he wasn't leaving.

"I want it. Now."

To avoid a scene, I handed it over. He left.

Thought that was the end of it.

Three months later, I'm walking through the store. See a familiar face at the promoter section.

It's him. Joining formalities. He'd been hired by one of our partner brands as a product promoter.

He saw me. Walked over.

“Sir.”

I nodded.

“I wanted to apologize. For that day. I was immature.”

I didn’t say anything. Just waited.

“I’ve learned since then.”

“Good. Welcome.”

He worked there for about six months. Did his job. Never brought it up again.

Most people don’t come back to apologize.

* * *

Part Two

Different interview. Mid-level position. Guy came in confident. Resume looked decent.

First round didn’t go well. Skills mismatch. Experience wasn’t what we needed.

I told him. “We’re not proceeding with your application.”

He nodded. Started packing his folder.

“Hold on,” I said.

He looked up.

"Your resume needs work. This section here, too vague. Mention specific achievements. Numbers. Results."

He listened.

"And this experience... doesn't align with what we're hiring for. But it could work for other roles. Focus on transferable skills when you apply elsewhere."

He was quiet. Then: "Can I ask why you're telling me this?"

I shrugged. "You're here anyway."

He smiled. "Sir, I've been to twelve interviews in two months. This is the first time anyone's given me feedback."

He shook my hand. Left.

* * *

Two rejections.

One came back angry, then apologetic.

One thanked me on the spot.

Chapter 3: Small Victories & Strange Moments

The Interview That Couldn't Happen on Tuesday

The Trainee Who Almost Quit

Excel: Yes. People: No.

The Gossip Alarm Clock

The Guy with Eight Dead Grandparents

Veg Guy Gets Non-Veg Sandwich

Aaj Ka Colour

The Back Call

CHAPTER 3

SMALL VICTORIES & STRANGE MOMENTS

The Interview That Couldn't Happen on Tuesday

Hiring. Decent candidate. Experience matched. References checked out.

HR called to schedule interview.

"Can you come Tuesday, 2 PM?"

"Tuesday is not possible, sir."

"Why? Are you busy?"

"No Sir, but Tuesday is Mangalvar. Not auspicious for starting new things. Interviews are new beginnings, no?"

I'm thinking: this is a job interview, not a wedding muhurat.

"Okay, what about Wednesday?"

"Wednesday is fine, sir. But I have some personal work that day."

"Thursday?"

"Thursday is perfect, Brihaspativar...very auspicious for career matters."

"Fine. Thursday, 2 PM."

"Sir, one more thing. Can we make it 2:30 PM instead? My pandit said after 2:15 is better for me personally."

Should I also check with your pandit about the questions I'll ask?

I didn't. Because I've been around long enough to know, you don't fight this battle.

"Sure. Thursday, 2:30."

He showed up Thursday at 2:30 sharp. Interview went well. Got hired.

First day of work, he asked: "Sir, which desk will be mine?"

I showed him. Corner desk, near the window.

He looked at it. Pulled out his phone. Opened a compass app.

"Sir, this desk is facing west. Can I get one facing east? East is good for career growth."

The other employees stared.

We didn't rearrange the office.

But he did put a Ganesha idol on his desk. And a brass tortoise. And a crystal pyramid.

"For positive energy, sir."

Worked with us for three years. One of our most punctual employees. Never late. Never absent.

On some days, he'd arrive on time, and do nothing new.

Can't argue with results.

Or astrology.

Or both.

The Trainee Who Almost Quit

Store 6. Issue escalated to me.

"Sir, trainee complained TL scolded him publicly. He's threatening to quit."

I called the trainee. Twenty-two years old. First job. On the verge of tears.

"What happened?"

"Sir, I made a small mistake with a customer's billing. TL shouted at me in front of everyone. Called me careless. I felt humiliated."

"Was it a small mistake or did the customer complain?"

"Customer didn't complain. I caught it myself and fixed it. But TL still yelled."

"In front of customers?"

"Yes, sir. In front of customers and other staff. Everyone was staring."

I could hear his voice shaking. Kid was genuinely hurt.

"Okay. Let me talk to the TL. Don't make any decisions yet."

I called the TL next. Thirty-something, been with the company for five years. Good at his job but had a temper.

"Why'd you shout at the trainee?"

"Sir, he's been making the same mistake for three days. I've told him politely twice already. Today I lost my patience."

"In front of customers?"

Pause. "Yes, sir."

"You know that's not okay, right? You want to correct him? Pull him aside. Don't humiliate him publicly."

"I was frustrated…"

"I get it. But you're the senior. He's learning. And now he wants to quit. Is that what you wanted?"

Longer pause. "No, sir. I didn't think he'd take it that hard."

"He's twenty-two. First job. You yelled at him in front of strangers. Of course he took it hard."

"I'll apologize, sir."

"Good. Do it properly. Not a half-hearted 'sorry if you felt bad' apology. Real sorry."

Next day, the TL walked up to the trainee during a quiet moment. No customers around.

"Hey. Can we talk?"

The trainee looked nervous. Nodded.

"I'm sorry about yesterday. I shouldn't have yelled at you like that. Especially not in front of customers."

The trainee looked down.

"You're learning. I forgot what that's like. I was frustrated, took it out on you. That's not fair."

It wasn't emotional.

Just awkward.

And that was enough

The trainee looked up. "It's okay, sir."

"It's not okay. But I'll do better. Ask me if you're stuck. I'll show you again."

They shook hands. Went back to work.

Later, I called the trainee to my desk.

"You still thinking about quitting?"

The trainee hesitated. "No, sir. I'll stay."

"Good. Next time you're stuck, ask. Everyone here screwed up when they started."

Two weeks later, the trainee had figured out the billing system.

No more errors.

Six months later, they were training new hires.

Excel: Yes. People: No.

Startup days. Interviewing for an MIS Executive role.

Nothing fancy. Excel, reports, numbers, accuracy.

The interview went well. Surprisingly well.

I gave him a trial task. He sent the report back the next day.

Clean. Structured. Sharp formulas.

One of those rare moments when you think… **haan, mil gaya**

We were almost done. Discussing joining date, salary confirmation.

Then, just before wrapping up, he asked quietly:

“Sir… does this job require me to talk to other departments for data?”

I said, “Sometimes. Not daily, but yes. If data doesn’t match, or something’s missing, you may need to follow up.”

He went silent for a few seconds.

Then he said, very calmly,

“Sorry sir. I can’t do that.”

I thought he was negotiating role clarity.

He continued,

“I have a problem speaking to people.”

I paused. “But you did well in the interview.”

He nodded.

"I know. It was very difficult."

I asked him, "Abhi naukri hai?"

"Nahi"

"So you need work?"

He looked at me. Didn't look away.

"Haan sir. Mujhe naukri chahiye."

Pause.

"But main baat nahi kar paunga."

That hit differently.

He wasn't walking away from a backup option. He had nothing. No job. No safety net.

And he was still saying no.

I tried once more.

"This is a good role. Close to your home. Exactly your skill set. The people interaction would be minimal, maybe once or twice a week."

He looked at me and said,

"Sir, you make me work on Excel for 12 hours, I will do it.

But speaking to people regularly… I won't be able to."

That was it.

He stood up, thanked me, and left.

No drama. No negotiation. No follow-up.

I sat there for a minute, staring at his resume.

Unemployed. Perfect skill match. Close to home. Desperate for work.

And he still walked away.

Because he knew better than most people with 5 years more experience, exactly where his line was.

I filled the role three weeks later. Different candidate. Less skilled with Excel, but comfortable with people.

That role needed both.

The first guy would've taken it, struggled silently for two months, then quit or got fired.

Instead, he saved us both the trouble.

By being honest when honesty cost him everything.

The Gossip Alarm Clock

Retail chain. Chai stall.

Two Department managers. Voices low.

"Heard the news?"

"What?"

"Big company's buying us. Takeover."

"Bullshit. Where'd you hear that?"

"Friend in finance. They're doing valuations."

I walked back to office. Regional Office sent an email that afternoon: "Team, some rumours are circulating. Ignore them. Business as usual."

Translation: It's true.

People started checking phones between meetings. LinkedIn profiles getting updated quietly.

I called a friend who'd been through a merger. "What happens to mid-level managers?"

"Update your CV."

I updated mine that night. Started applying the next week.

Three months later: announcement. Merger confirmed. Restructuring. My role? Eliminated.

But I already had interviews lined up.

The people who waited for the official memo? Scrambling.

Turns out the chai stall was more reliable than corporate communications.

The Guy with Eight Dead Grandparents

We had this floor staff guy at the retail chain. Let's call him Ravi.

Sharp worker. Good with customers. Never late.

But every month, without fail, something happened.

Month one: Grandmother.

Month two: Uncle.

Month three: Cousin's accident.

By month four, I'm noticing a pattern.

'Ravi, how many grandparents do you have?"

He didn't even hesitate. "Four, sir. Mother's side, father's side. Plus wife's side, that's eight total."

"And how many have passed away this year?"

"This is number three, sir."

Technically possible. Couldn't argue.

Month five: Another uncle.

Month six: Wife's grandmother.

Month seven: Distant cousin.

By month eight, the other staff started a betting pool. "Who's dying this month?"

One guy joked, "At this rate, his whole village will be over by year-end"

I pulled him aside once. "Ravi, real talk. Are all these real?"

He looked genuinely offended. "Sir, you think I'm lying? Main jhooth nahi bolta, sir."

"I'm not saying that. I'm saying it's... a lot of deaths in one year."

"Sir, big family. Joint family hai gaon mein. Pachaas–saath log. Jab kisi ka death hota hai, sabko jaana padta hai. Yahi hamara rivaaj hai."

Fair point. I couldn't argue with culture.

Month nine: Another relative.

I told him: "Ravi, you've used up all your casual leave and most of your earned leave. Next time, it's unpaid."

"Understood, sir."

Month ten: "Sir, aunt passed..."

"Unpaid leave, Ravi."

"Ji, sir."

He took it. No complaints. Came back. Worked hard.

The thing is? He never actually screwed up at work. Always delivered when he was there. Never gave attitude.

So either: A) He had the unluckiest family in India, or B) He had relatives in every village within 500 kilometres.

I never figured out which.

But Ravi survived. Outlasted three managers, including me.

Veg Guy Gets Non-Veg Sandwich

Late evening. Room service. Order comes in: Club sandwich, vegetarian, Room 512.

Kitchen prepares it. Steward delivers it.

Ten minutes later, my phone rings. Guest in 512. Furious.

"I'm a strict vegetarian. I ordered a veg club sandwich. You sent me chicken."

My brain froze.

If he'd taken a bite, this would've been a full-blown crisis. Religious sentiments. Complaint to management. Maybe legal issues.

I rushed to his room. Apologized profusely. "Sir, I'm so sorry. This is completely our fault. We'll prepare a fresh veg sandwich immediately and send it up. Your entire meal is complimentary."

He was upset but calmed down when he realized we were taking it seriously. Thankfully, he hadn't bitten into it yet, had just opened the sandwich to check and saw the chicken.

Disaster averted by sheer luck.

Back in the kitchen, I found the steward who'd delivered it. He looked exhausted.

"What happened?"

"Sir, I was sleepy. There were two orders, one veg, one non-veg. The non-veg got ready first. I thought it was the only order and just took it up."

He hadn't checked the KOT (order slip). Just grabbed the first sandwich that appeared on the counter and delivered it.

I checked with the kitchen. They'd prepared both sandwiches. Had them clearly labelled. Veg on one tray, non-veg on another.

But the steward hadn't looked at the labels.

"How long have you been on shift?"

"Since 6 AM, sir. It's almost 11 PM now."

Seventeen-hour shift. No wonder he was making mistakes.

But the immediate problem: we'd almost served meat to a strict vegetarian.

Made the meal free. Sent a fruit basket. Guest checked out the next day without further complaints.

After that, delivery wasn't about speed. It was about verification. Order slip checked. Label checked. Only then did food leave the kitchen

The steward who made the mistake? Transferred to a different shift. Seventeen-hour days stopped for him too.

After that, I stopped trusting "it'll be fine."

Aaj Ka Colour

It was a traditional startup. The kind where every sentence ended with "ji.".

One morning, I reached office and felt… odd. Not immediately. Slowly.

Everyone was wearing yellow.

Yellow shirts. Yellow kurtis. Different shades, same family.

I was the only one not invited to the theme.

Didn't think much of it till late morning.

Then I asked a colleague.

"Aaj koi special day hai kya?"

He looked at me. "Kyun?"

"Maine notice kiya… aaj sab peele shades mein hain. Koi tyohar hai kya?"

He burst out laughing.

"Aaj Brihaspativaar hai. Isliye peela pehente hain."

"Oh." Then, genuinely curious, "Baaki din ka bhi koi colour hota hai kya?"

He smiled. "Aap observe karo. Khud pata chal jayega."

So I did.

Monday - mostly white.

Tuesday - red trying very hard to be maroon.

Thursday - yellow, without fail.

Friday - something between pastel and belief.

Different shades. Same intention.

Like a school uniform, but with faith.

Later, someone explained it properly.

Each day. One colour. One grah.

Initially, I wasn't keen.

Mera system simple tha…jo almirah ke saamne dikha, wahi pehno.

But slowly, it got to me.

On Wednesdays, I started pausing.

On Thursdays, checking twice.

By Friday, I was matching…almost unconsciously.

No one told me to.

No email. No policy. No reminder.

The colours did the work.

The Back Call

Punjab.

Warehouse role interviews.

Candidate from Ludhiana.

Interview done.

Decent.

Not brilliant.

Not terrible.

I said, "We'll get back to you."

He nodded.

Next morning, my phone rang.

‘Sir, backcall nahi aya.”

I paused.

“Backcall?”

“Haan ji. Aapne bola tha backcall karenge.”

“No, no” I said. That just means we’ll inform you later. When we decide.”

Pause.

“Toh abhi bata dijiye…”

Fair point.

“Backcall,” to him, meant a scheduled callback.

To me it was corporate politeness.

Same sentence.

Different expectations.

After that, I stopped saying “we’ll get back to you.”

Started saying:

“Agar select hue, call karenge.”

Just the selected ones.

Not everyone else.

PART TWO

BUILDING SYSTEMS (OR TRYING TO)

Chapter 4: Learning in the Middle Lane

The Day I Accidentally Published the Co-Founder's Salary

The ₹3 Lakh Soap Mystery

When Excel Had to Retire

The HR System That Came With Free Promises

CHAPTER 4

LEARNING IN THE MIDDLE LANE

The Day I Accidentally Published the Co-Founder's Salary

I was new at the company. Fresh into the role. Still learning the email groups.

One afternoon, I needed to send salary data to the HR leadership team.

Simple task. Attach Excel file, send to "HR Leadership."

Except I didn't send it to "HR Leadership."

I sent it to "All HO Staff."

The Excel file contained everyone's salary. Including the co-founder's.

Ten minutes later, my inbox exploded.

"Is this meant for us?"

"Should we have access to this?"

Someone forwarded a screenshot.

The co-founder's salary.

Multiple question marks.

My stomach dropped.

Screenshots.

Whispers.

Side-eyes.

Faster than Swiggy notifications.

Things I heard later:

"Yeh banda mujhe se zyada kya karta hai?"

"Boss ka salary dekh ke BP high ho gaya."

"I'm underpaid. Or he's overpaid. I don't know anymore."

I called my manager.

"I sent the salary file to everyone."

Long pause. "Everyone?"

"Everyone."

Another pause.

"Including ...?"

"Yes."

"Come to my cabin. Now."

I sent a follow-up email asking everyone to delete the file.

Nobody deleted it.

Leadership held an emergency meeting. "How Did This Happen?"

I knew the answer.

One wrong click.

One wrong mailing list.

The co-founder chose not to make it an issue.

Maybe because I was new.

Maybe because he had perspective.

Maybe because the damage was already done.

Maybe because he knew I'd never do it again

For the next six months, every time I attached a file, I checked the recipient list five times.

I Still do.

The ₹3 Lakh Soap Mystery

We started getting bulk returns. Same product: soap. Same complaint: "Box short by a few pieces."

Losses: ₹2 lakhs. Then ₹3 lakhs.

The boxes looked perfect. Company tape sealed. No tampering.

I called a meeting. "What's going on?"

Receiving supervisor: "Sir, we count every carton. Piece by piece. Nothing's missing when we receive it."

"Then how are traders returning short boxes?"

"Maybe they're removing pieces themselves. Then claiming it was short. Taking advantage of our return policy."

"With company tape still sealed?"

Silence.

"Let's check the next consignment. Physically. Open random boxes."

Next delivery comes in. Fifty cartons. We pick five randomly.

Box one: Open it. Count. 72 soaps. Correct.

Box two: Count. 72 soaps. Correct.

Box three: Same. Perfect.

By box four, we were just going through the motions. Everyone was tired

Then the junior-most GR (Goods receiving) guy, quiet kid, maybe 23, barely says two words normally, speaks up.

"Sir, let's empty one completely. Take all the soaps out."

Everyone looked at him. "We already counted them."

"I know. But let's see the layers."

We humoured him. Started pulling bars out. Top layer, all there. Arranged neatly.

Next layer down, missing. An entire layer. Gone.

We stared.

The top layer had been arranged in a crisscross pattern. Made it look full from above. But underneath? Empty space.

"How the hell did someone do this with company tape still sealed?"

We checked the seal closely. Company tape. Correct logo. Correct adhesive. No signs of tampering.

We found the crisscross trick. That explained the returns.

But the losses kept happening. New batches, same problem.

Someone suggested weighing cartons instead of just counting. Weights didn't match.

That's when one loader quietly mentioned: truck guys carried extra tape rolls "for sealing on the way."

They were stopping at dhabas. Opening boxes. Taking pieces. Resealing. Selling in grey market.

Transporter got changed. Supplier controlled the tapes.

Shortage stopped overnight.

When Excel Had to Retire

Small fashion startup. Growing fast. No systems.

Payroll ran on Excel. One sheet, one guy, and everyone tiptoeing around him near salary day.

If he was absent, payroll stalled. If a formula broke, the whole cycle froze.

Come salary week, nobody dared disturb him…like he was guarding the nation's gold reserves.

Then, on the 29th, the Excel guy, Mohan, called in sick.

The founder called me.

"Mohan's not coming. Can you handle payroll? I must release the salary tomorrow."

"Payroll execution sat with Mohan. I'd only reviewed outputs."

"Just open it and follow the formulas."

I opened it. A jungle of tabs. Formulas referencing formulas, some I didn't even understand.

Tab 1: Employee master data. Tab 2: Attendance. Tab 3: Leave adjustments. Somewhere at the end: the final calculation.

I called Mohan.

"Walk me through this."

He coughed.

"Sir... copy last month's sheet... update attendance... run the final calculation tab..."

"Which tab?"

He hesitated. "The last one... buried at the end."

Of course it was.

Four hours later, I got it working. Sent the payment file to the founder.

He called back.

"Last month's payroll was around ₹4.5 lakh and this month about ₹4.8 lakh... we haven't hired anyone new. Something seems off."

I fixed a missed deduction, resent it, and salaries went out on time. Barely.

Next day, I went to the founder.

"This Excel system is a disaster. One guy gets sick and the whole thing falls apart."

He nodded.

"Let's fix it now."

The HR System That Came With Free Promises

Let's put an HR system in place.

Founder said, "Get the best option. Not too expensive. Solid."

So I did what one does when asked to "get the best."

Spoke to five-six vendors. Sat through demos so long I started confusing leave management with payroll and payroll with astrology.

Every vendor said the same thing:

"This feature is optional."

"That module is coming next quarter."

"This problem will disappear once you go live."

I made a comparison table. Features. Costs. Pros. Cons. Support. Implementation timeline.

Excel at its finest.

Sent it to the founder. Waited.

Then the co-founder said, "Let's go with Sanjay's."

Founder asked, "Cost?"

It was the most expensive one on the list.

I resent the comparison. Highlighted the gaps in Sanjay's system.

Co-founder said, "Sanjay has connects. He'll get us business."

Founder said, "Okay."

That was the decision.

My Excel comparison? Appreciated. Then ignored.

Six months later, the business never came.

What did come:

Random notifications at 3 AM.

Customer support that didn't respond.

No call centre.

An implementation manual that assumed you were also the product manager.

We did everything ourselves. Data migration. User training. Troubleshooting. All of it.

The cheaper system we'd rejected? I checked their website one day. Client testimonials. Case studies. "Works out of the box."

Sanjay's system? Still described as "in early stage."

Eventually, nobody mentioned the HR system again.

Which, I suppose, meant it had successfully blended into the company culture.

Like most decisions made on "connects."

Chapter 5: When Nobody Reports to You But Everyone's Your Problem

Section A: Managing Without Authority

The 6 AM Employee Revolt

The Scheduling System Nobody Wanted

The Ghost on Payroll

The Zoho Pitch That Almost Didn't Happen

CHAPTER 5

WHEN NOBODY REPORTS TO YOU BUT EVERYONE'S YOUR PROBLEM

SECTION A: MANAGING WITHOUT AUTHORITY

The 6 AM Employee Revolt

6 AM. My phone rang. Store supervisor-panicking.

"Sir, employees at the store have refused to work and aren't letting other employees in to open."

I was half-asleep. "What? Why?"

"They're saying they won't work until their demands are met."

"What demands?"

"I don't know. They won't talk to me. They want to talk to you."

I threw on clothes, rushed to the store. About twelve employees standing outside, blocking the entrance. Another five employees who'd come to open the store were standing awkwardly to the side.

I walked up. "What's going on?"

One guy, older than the rest, stepped forward. "Sir, we're not working until our issues are resolved."

"What issues?"

"Our supervisor has been mistreating us. Verbal abuse. Favouritism. Threatening with job loss. We've complained multiple times. Nothing happened."

"Give me examples."

They did. Supervisor yelling at people publicly. Giving good shifts to his favourites. Overloading others with extra work. Threatening to fire anyone who dared speak up. Classic toxic boss behaviour.

"Why didn't you escalate this?"

"We did, sir. Store manager said he'd handle it. Nothing changed."

I looked at the store manager. He looked uncomfortable.

"Can we go inside and discuss this?"

The older employee shook his head. "No, sir. Last time we 'discussed,' nothing happened. This time we're not moving until we see action."

Fair point.

I called the regional manager. Explained the situation. He said he'd come immediately.

Meanwhile, I sat down on the sidewalk with them. "Okay. I'm listening. Tell me everything."

They did. Took about forty-five minutes. By the end, I had a clear picture. The supervisor was a nightmare. And the store manager had been covering for him because they were friends.

Regional manager arrived. We had a quick huddle. Decided: suspend the supervisor pending investigation.

I went back to the employees. "Supervisor is suspended effective immediately. Investigation will happen. Good enough?"

They talked among themselves. Then nodded.

"We'll work. But if nothing changes, we'll walk out permanently."

"Fair."

They went inside. Store opened. Crisis averted.

The supervisor? Investigation confirmed everything. He was transferred. He got transferred, problem solved, at least in my stores.

Crisis management, as it turns out, is mostly about showing up.

The Scheduling System Nobody Wanted

The email came from Germany.

Subject: "Implementation of Workforce Optimization System – Mandatory"

Our parent company's head office had analysed our scheduling data. Conclusion: we were overstaffed during slow hours, understaffed during rush hours. Labour costs were up. Customer complaints were up.

Solution: new scheduling software. Built in Germany. Tested in Germany. Rolled out to Germany.

Now being forced upon India.

What looked like inefficiency to Germany was survival to us.

Their retail ran on patterns. Ours ran on mood, festivals, rumours, and WhatsApp forwards.

But Germany had data. And data always wins meetings.

The system matched staff to footfall patterns.

Peak hours got people. Slow hours didn't.

Simple. Efficient. Very German.

Problem? Indian retail doesn't follow patterns. German stores are predictable. Indian stores are chaos.

Random festival? Footfall spike. Long weekend announced last-minute? Footfall spike. EOSS rumors? Footfall spike.

But Germany had decided. So we had to implement.

Selling the Unsellable

I called a meeting with my team. Fifteen people. Store managers, team leads, floor supervisors.

Announced the new system.

Two minutes in, Ramesh raised his hand. "Sir, why are we changing? Current system works fine."

I could've said, "Germany wants this."

Would've been honest. Would've also made me sound like I had no spine.

Instead, I closed my laptop. "Let me show you something."

I pulled up last month's roster data on the projector.

"Saturday evening, 6 PM. Rush hour. Forty customers in billing queue. How many people did we have on the floor?"

Ramesh checked his notes. "Four, sir."

"Four. For forty customers. How long did people wait?"

"Twenty minutes average."

"Right. Now, same day, 11 AM. Slow hour. Ten customers total. How many staff?"

"Seven, sir."

"Seven people standing around for ten customers. Meanwhile, evening shift is drowning."

I clicked to the next slide. Ramesh's schedule from last month.

"Ramesh, remember those six straight weekends you worked? You were ready to murder me."

He laughed. "I was, sir."

"This system? It would've flagged that automatically. I couldn't have screwed you even if I tried."

The room got quieter.

"Anyone else have scheduling nightmares last month?"

Several hands went up. Night shifts followed by morning shifts. Random off days. Split shifts that wasted entire days.

I showed them how the system would prevent those problems. Automatic flags. Clustered off days. Minimum gaps between shifts.

But more importantly, matched staff to actual customer volume. Busy hours = more people. Slow hours = fewer people standing around bored.

Suddenly it wasn't "Germany's policy." It was "the thing that stops us from drowning during rush hour while also stopping Ramesh from working every damn weekend."

By the end, they weren't fighting it, they were asking when we'd start.

Implementation Chaos

Day one, my phone exploded.

"Sir, system won't let me schedule Anil."

"Did you save after deleting his night shift?"

Pause. "Oh."

By day three, the calls reduced. By week two, the system was running smoothly.

Two weeks later, Ramesh came to my desk.

"Sir, I got next month's schedule. All my off days are weekends. First time in six months."

He paused. "I take back everything I said in that meeting."

When Germany Met Diwali

The system worked. For three months, it worked beautifully.

Then Diwali season hit.

German algorithm had analysed our footfall data. Predicted patterns. Optimised staffing.

What it didn't predict: India's collective decision to shop like the world was ending.

Thursday afternoon, normal day according to the system. Scheduled staff: six people.

Actual footfall: triple the usual. Some random influencer posted about our Diwali sale. Post went viral.

We were drowning.

I called everyone I could. "Can you come in? Emergency."

Half showed up. We survived. Barely.

Next day, I sent feedback to HO: "System works for predictable markets. Need manual override option for festivals and acts of God."

Reply came two weeks later: "Override function will be added in next update. Thank you for feedback."

Very polite.

The override function arrived four months later. By then, we'd already figured out our own jugaad…keeping a few people on "standby" during festival season, just in case.

Germany had given us efficiency. We added flexibility.

That's how it works here. Take the system. Make it survive India.

The Ghost on Payroll

The store had access cards.

One guy figured out a shortcut.

Give his card to a buddy.

Buddy swipes him in.

Meanwhile, the first guy sipped chai somewhere else.

Weeks passed.

One day, the store manager did rounds and asked,

"Where's Rahul?"

Supervisor shrugged: "I thought he left..."

"But his attendance shows he is present today!"

CCTV told a different story.

I called both of them to my office. Rahul and his buddy, Sameer.

"Explain this"

Rahul stared at the floor.

Sameer stared at the wall.

"I'm waiting."

Sameer spoke first.

"Sir, Rahul had some personal work. I was just helping a friend."

"For how long?"

Silence.

"How. Long."

"Two weeks, sir."

"Two weeks you didn't come to work, and he swiped you in?"

"Sir, I had family issues…"

"Did you apply for leave?"

"No"

"Why not?"

"I didn't have leave balance"

"So instead of unpaid leave chose fraud."

Rahul flinched.

"Sir, I needed the salary…"

"For work you didn't do?"

Silence.

I looked at Sameer.

"Help is lending him money.

Help is covering his shift.

Help is not attendance fraud."

They were suspended pending investigation.

Both were terminated a week later.

After that, I started checking CCTV randomly.

Not daily.

Unpredictably.

The ghost employee problem disappeared.

The Zoho Pitch That Almost Didn't Happen

I suggested moving to an HRMS. Scouted options. Ran trials.

The founder nodded.

Then nothing happened.

Weeks passed. "We're thinking about it."

More weeks. Still nothing.

Finally, I asked, "Why aren't we moving on this?"

He hesitated. "We already have Zoho."

I stared. "And you're still running payroll on Excel?"

"We use Zoho for accounts. Didn't realize it had payroll."

I wanted to scream. Paying for a tool and still calculating salaries in Excel?

Like owning a car and taking the bus because you forgot the car exists.

"Let's use Zoho Payroll. I'll set it up."

He agreed. Finally.

The Excel Guy Who Didn't Trust Zoho

Mohan wasn't thrilled.

He trusted Excel, not a dashboard he didn't understand.

First cycle was painful. Uploading data, setting up salary structures.

"Excel says ₹45,000. Zoho says ₹45,200."

"Where's the ₹200 difference?"

Zoho had calculated a component Excel missed.

"So Zoho's accurate?"

"Looks like it."

Salary day was tense. I clicked "Process Payroll" like defusing a bomb.

System processed. Sent to bank.

Next day, salaries hit accounts. No missing amounts. No panic calls.

Mohan looked at the dashboard. "This works."

"Told you."

By the third month on Zoho:

"Sir, I finished payroll in two hours today."

"Good."

"Usually six on Excel."

He smiled. First time I'd seen it in three months.

A month later, the founder called:

"How much time is Zoho saving?"

"Mohan used to spend six hours on payroll. Now it's two. Plus fewer errors, better audit trail."

"What else can we automate?"

"Leave, attendance, performance appraisals. We're barely using 10% of what we pay for."

"Set it up."

Three months later, rollout complete. Team grumbled at first. Two months later, nobody wanted to go back.

Six months later, Mohan had become the Zoho expert. New employee questions? "Ask Mohan." Reports? "Mohan will pull it."

From Excel warrior to cloud expert. Not bad.

Section B: Absurd Systems & Leadership

Five-Year Plans vs. Arial Font

The Blind Zone

The Missing Vowel Apology

When Astrology Delayed Resignations

Four Bananas, Immediate Consumption

The KRA Meeting That Took Five Hours

The Encyclopaedia Nobody Opened

Global Best Practices... Local "Ji" Update

The WhatsApp Engagement War

Good Ideas Travel. Credit Doesn't.

Midnight Updates, Morning Backstab

The Resignation That Hurt Feelings

SECTION B: ABSURD SYSTEMS & LEADERSHIP

Five-Year Plans vs. Arial Font

Startup days.

Big conference room. Day-long presentations. Every department head rolling out five-year plans.

Sales went first. Slides. Excel sheets. Growth curves stretching confidently to the right.

The founder sat in the front row. Listening. Face unreadable.

Marketing followed. Market expansion. Revenue projections. Big words delivered with bigger confidence.

The founder asked one question. "How do you plan to execute this?"

They answered. He nodded.

Then HR. Then Tech. Everyone was ready.

"Scalability."

"Synergies."

"Growth trajectory."

The founder listened to everything.

Feedback time.

The first presenter waited for strategy. Direction. Validation.

The founder leaned forward.

"In this sheet… these two columns look different."

Silence.

“They should look the same. Please fix that.”

The presenter blinked. “Yes, sir.”

Next presentation.

“Slide three. The heading isn’t aligned properly.”

A quick nod. “I’ll correct it.”

Third presentation.

By now, the room was uneasy.

People opened laptops mid-session.

Margins checked. Fonts scanned. Alignment adjusted.

Not assumptions. Not plans. Just formatting

Someone whispered behind me, “Arial and Calibri.”

By lunch, nobody was thinking about five-year plans anymore.

They were thinking about spacing.

Only after the corrections were made did the founder move on to content.

Questions were sharp. Feedback was clear. Assumptions were challenged.

But the damage was done.

By the end of the day, one thing was crystal clear.

Nobody remembered the strategies.

Nobody remembered the projections.

But every Excel sheet?

Perfectly formatted.

The Blind Zone

There was a founder who loved CCTV cameras.

Not for security. For comfort.

His comfort. Not ours.

Cameras were everywhere, office rooms, work areas, corners that didn't need corners.

And he watched them. Constantly.

Every few minutes, he'd call.

"Come. See this."

He'd pause the footage like it was a crime documentary.

"Your banda is laughing," he'd say. "Kaam nahin kar raha hai."

I'd look at the screen.

The guy was sitting at his desk. File open. Laptop on.

Smiling.

That was the crime.

In real life, this employee was one of the smartest, sharpest performers we had. Delivered on time. No drama. No excuses.

But on camera…he'd committed the sin of looking happy.

I wanted to say: "He's smiling WHILE working. That's actually a good sign."

I didn't. Because the founder didn't want explanations. He wanted seriousness. On screen. At all times.

After a few such calls, I figured it out.

He wasn't worried about productivity.

He was worried about optics.

The message went around.

"If you have to talk, laugh, or breathe deeply,do it in the blind zone."

They looked at me.

"The blind zone?"

"The area the camera doesn't cover. Five minutes max. Then come back looking busy. Otherwise he'll panic."

One guy asked, "What if there's no blind zone?"

"There's always a blind zone. Find it. Use it. Return looking stressed."

After that, people worked.

People laughed.

People disappeared briefly.

And returned looking appropriately miserable.

The cameras were satisfied.

The founder was calm.

Work continued.

That was the system.

The Missing Vowel Apology.

Retail chain days. Regional manager, let's call him Devendra.

Particular about two things: punctuality and spelling his name correctly.

One day, junior employee sent him an email.

Subject line: "Store 5 Monthly Report – Attached"

Work was solid. Except one thing.

Email started: "Dear Devender Sir,"

One missing "a."

Now, to be fair, there WAS another senior in the company called Devender. Marketing head. Same floor.

So the junior wasn't being careless. Just surrounded by too many Devens.

Devendra noticed.

Not the report. The vowel.

He replied within ten minutes.

Not with corrections to the report. Not with "good work" or "noted."

Just: "It's Devendra. Not Devender. Please send an apology email."

The junior panicked. Called me.

"Sir, what do I do?"

"Apologise. Fast. Move on."

He sent: "Sorry sir for the oversight."

Devendra replied: "This isn't a proper apology. Send a formal email with subject line. CC your team lead."

The junior stared at his screen.

He'd spent two days compiling that report. Checked every number. Cross-referenced with finance.

The vowel mattered.

He drafted the apology.

Subject: Apology for Error in Name

Dear Devendra Sir,

I sincerely apologise for incorrectly spelling your name as "Devender" in my previous email. This was an unintentional oversight on my part. I regret the error and will ensure it does not happen again.

Regards,

[Name]

Sent. CC'd team lead. CC'd me.

Devendra replied: "Accepted. Moving forward, please be more careful."

The junior called me again.

"Sir, is this normal?"

"Define normal."

After that, he triple-checked every email. Not the numbers. The names.

Work continued.

Devendra felt respected.

***

Different startup. Different founder.

This one was called Sourav.

His email ID was clear: sourav@company.com

For the first few months, vendors and partners kept writing back:

"Dear Saurab,"

Business contacts. Consultants.

They saw his email signature.

They saw the email address.

Still wrote Saurab.

Because that's how they said it. Natural pronunciation. Habit.

First month, Sourav corrected people politely.

"It's Sourav, by the way."

They apologised.

"Sorry, typo."

"Sorry, autocorrect."

"Sorry, mistake."

Next email?

Back to Saurab.

He corrected again. Same cycle.

By the third month, he'd corrected seven different people.

By the fourth month, he stopped.

Too many Saurabs in too many inboxes.

So he just… let it go.

But you could see it.

In meetings, someone would say, "Saurab…"

He'd pause. Just a fraction.

Then continue.

Permanently annoyed. Quietly defeated.

When Astrology Delayed Resignations

When I joined this startup, the head of Sales and Marketing had just resigned.

Good guy. Underpaid. Live deals hanging. No handover.

The founder asked me to convince him to serve his full notice period.

I called him to my cabin. Polite. Calm. Professional. Explained the situation.

He listened. Called the founder. Founder also requested.

He came back. Visibly disturbed.

Not because of workload.

Not because of targets.

Because of muhurat.

"Sir... maine company join karne se pehle apne Guruji se baat karke date aur time fix karaya tha."

I nodded. Confused.

"Ab dobara poochna padega. Kab accha muhurat hoga next joining ke liye. Agar muhurat sahi nahi hua... toh gadbad ho jayegi."

No jokes. Pure fear.

Up till then, my career had involved toxic founders, salary meltdowns, midnight layoffs.

But never astrology-driven notice periods.

Later I realized this wasn't just him.

People preferred joining only on Wednesdays.

Offer letters signed on Monday.

Background checks by Tuesday.

Actual joining... Wednesday.

Then came the seating plan.

The company didn't allocate desks.

They allocated directions.

Founder in the power corner.

Finance in the north. Sales facing east.

HR - wherever the Wi-Fi was weakest.

Perfect muhurats.

Perfect Vastu.

Everything aligned.

Despite every perfectly chosen date and direction, the company shut down.

Smoothly.

Silently.

Without checking with Guruji.

Four Bananas, Immediate Consumption

Large retail chain. Work trip to Jaipur.

My boss believed in astrology, vastu, signs from the universe.

Harmless, mostly. Until it wasn't.

Before we reached the store, he stopped the car and bought bananas.

About half a dozen.

I didn't ask why.

If a senior buys something without explanation, you're not part of the story.

We reached the store.

Work happened.

Around lunchtime, he suddenly walked out.

No announcement. No reason.

I followed. Reflex.

Our store was at a busy Jaipur crossing.

Traffic, noise, people everywhere.

My boss scanned the road like he was looking for a cab.

Then he spotted a man, shabbily dressed, probably a daily-wage labourer.

He called him over.

"Kela khayega?"

The man nodded. Obviously.

My boss handed him four bananas.

The man smiled, took them, and started walking away…happy, confused, but happy.

That's when my boss froze.

Something had occurred to him.

He shouted, "Arre… idhar aao!"

The labourer came back.

My boss looked at him seriously and said,

"Yahin khao."

The man stared. Blank.

My boss continued, slightly irritated now,

"Mujhe kaise pata chalega tumne khaya ya kisi aur ko de diya?"

The poor guy panicked.

"Nahi babu… main hi khaunga."

"Abhi. Yahin."

And so, standing at a busy Jaipur crossing, under supervision, the man ate all four bananas. One after another.

Once the fourth banana disappeared, he nodded. Satisfied.

The labourer wiped his mouth and left.

Still confused. Still polite.

My boss turned around and walked back to the store.

No explanation.

I didn't ask.

The KRA Meeting That Took Five Hours

We started at 2 PM. Just me and the founder in his tiny cabin.

"Let's start with Priya. What's her role?"

"Sales."

"Okay. What does good sales performance look like for Priya specifically?"

He thought. "She should... sell stuff?"

I sighed. "How much stuff? To how many customers? What's a realistic monthly target?"

"I don't know. Maybe... ₹5 lakhs?"

"Based on what? Last month she did ₹3 lakhs. Month before, ₹4 lakhs. You're asking her to jump to ₹5 lakhs without any change in territory or resources."

He scratched his head. "Okay, maybe ₹4.5 lakhs?"

"Why ₹4.5 lakhs?"

"It's between ₹4 and ₹5?"

I took a breath.

"Let's approach this differently. What's the average monthly sales across your entire team?"

He pulled up a spreadsheet. "About ₹3.8 lakhs per person."

"Okay. So Priya's already above average. Good performer. Let's set her target at ₹4.2 lakhs, reasonable stretch but achievable."

He nodded. "That makes sense."

We spent the next four hours going through every single person. Sales targets. Customer retention metrics. Response times. Quality checks.

By 7 PM, we had a complete KRA sheet for everyone.

The founder looked exhausted. "This is a lot of work."

"You only have to do it once a year."

"What if someone's performance changes mid-year?"

"Then you have a mid-year review. Adjust targets if needed."

He saved the document. "This feels... structured."

"That's the idea."

Three Months Later

Performance review season.

I opened the KRA document. Started pulling up each person's numbers against their targets.

Priya: ₹4.3 lakhs average. Exceeded target.

Karthik: ₹3.5 lakhs. Below target, but improving.

Rahul: ₹5.2 lakhs. Crushing it.

Called the founder.

"Ready for performance reviews? I've got everyone's numbers against their KRAs."

"Oh. About that. I've already decided who's getting increments."

I paused. "Based on what?"

"Gut feeling. Who I think did well."

"We have actual data now. Numbers. Targets they hit or missed."

"Yeah, but I know my people. I can tell who's performing."

I looked at the spreadsheet. Five hours of work. Every target carefully calculated.

"So... we're not using the KRAs?"

"They're good to have. For reference. But I prefer to go with my instinct."

I closed my laptop.

Next quarter, he asked me to update the KRA sheet.

I did. Took another three hours.

He saved it. I never saw him touch it again.

The document lived in a folder titled "HR - Important."

Right next to the salary benchmarking report he'd asked for and never read.

The Encyclopaedia Nobody Opened

The retail chain. I asked my boss for the operations manual.

"I need to understand the processes. Instead of running around asking random people how things work."

She looked at me. "There isn't one."

"No manual?"

"No."

Few weeks later, store visit. Store manager's office. Shelf in the corner.

There it is. Thick book. Encyclopaedia-level thick. Covered in dust.

I pulled it out. Wiped the cover. Flipped through.

Store opening procedures. Closing procedures. Cash reconciliation. Staff scheduling. Inventory management. Customer complaints. Emergency protocols. Everything documented. Hundreds of pages.

Half the content wasn't even relevant anymore. Outdated processes. Old systems. Policies that had changed years ago.

"Do you have an updated version?" I asked the SM.

He laughed. "That is the version. External agency made it. Charged a bomb. Big launch event. Pomp and show. Then... nothing. Never got implemented."

I flipped to a random page. 'End of Day Cash Reconciliation' - twelve steps, three Excel templates, sign-offs from four people.

Problem? Our stores closed at 11 PM. By the time you followed those twelve steps, it was 1 AM.

So people just... did it the old way. Wrote numbers in a register. Got it signed by whoever was around. Done in ten minutes.

The manual's way was perfect. Our way happened.

Then COVID hit. Lockdowns. Reopening protocols. Social distancing. Sanitization schedules. Contactless payments.

Every process changed. Overnight.

The manual? Still on the shelf. Now covering pre-COVID operations that literally didn't exist anymore.

Nobody updated it. Nobody was using it anyway.

Regional meeting. My boss presenting operational improvements.

Senior VP asked: "Don't we already have an operations manual? I remember approving budget for that years ago."

My boss froze. 'Uh... yes, sir. We have one."

"Good. So we're following it?"

"We're... reviewing it for updates."

"How long does a review take?"

Silence.

After the meeting, my boss gave me the manual. I could tell it wasn't going to see the light of day

Q3 came and went. No updated manual.

Next year, new VP joined. Never asked about the manual.

The book stayed on the shelf. Perfect processes. Zero implementation.

Somewhere in that encyclopaedia was probably a twelve-step SOP for updating the encyclopaedia.

Global Best Practices… Local "Ji" Update

I had joined a brand-new startup in Jaipur.

Young founder.

Big dreams.

Slides full of "global best practices."

Perfect.

After years in MNCs, I was used to first-name culture.

No sir.

No boss.

Definitely no "ji."

Just plain names.

Day 1:

Founder: "Welcome, Arup! Call me Rohan."

Great start.

Day 2:

Staff walks in:

"Arup ji, chai le lijiye."

I let it pass.

Day 3:

"Arup ji, meeting start ho gayi."

"Arup ji, payroll check kar dena."

"Arup ji, file aapke table pe rakh di."

By Day 4, housekeeping joined the movement:

"Arup ji, pantry clean kar diya."

Somewhere between global best practices and local habits, my name got a cultural upgrade.

The best part?

One afternoon, even the founder, Mr Global Best Practices himself, walked in and casually said:

"Arup ji, woh presentation dekh li?"

At that moment, I realised it wasn't an accident.

It was Jaipur's default setting.

Within a week:

Emails had "Arup ji."

WhatsApp messages had "Arup ji."

This startup had big dreams of going international,

but the culture had already decided to go deeply, proudly local.

The WhatsApp Engagement War

Early WhatsApp days. No forwards yet. No "Good Morning" with sunrise GIFs. Just actual work communication.

My boss had an idea: "Let's make a group for all store HRs. Share employee engagement activities in real time."

Sounded reasonable.

Company KRA: employee engagement. Every store had weekly activities. Sports day, rangoli competition, team lunch. Standard stuff.

I thought the challenge would be getting employees to participate.

Wrong.

The challenge was managing the HR photo race.

Every activity ended the same way: HRs scrambling to click photos. Not of employees. Of banners. Balloons. Maybe one blurry crowd shot.

Then the race to post first in the WhatsApp group.

Why? If you posted first, the boss might like your photo. And if he liked it, that was a gold star for appraisal season

The group became a warzone.

Store 2 HR: Posted at 2:14 PM. Two likes. Boss included.

Store 4 HR: Posted at 2:16 PM. One like. Not from boss.

Next day, Store 4 HR called.

"Sir, why didn't boss like my photo?"

"Maybe he didn't see it."

"But he liked Store 2's! Mine had better participation!"

I looked. Both photos had maybe ten people. Same blurry quality, same bad lighting.

"I don't think the boss is analysing crowd size."

"Then why not mine?"

"Maybe he was busy."

Some HRs sulked. Others messaged me privately: "I posted first but got fewer likes. Is something wrong with my activities?"

I wanted to say: 'You're worried about WhatsApp likes. That's what's wrong."

Instead: "Your activities are fine. Focus on actual participation."

Next activity, same thing. Photo race. Like counting. Silent competition.

Some HRs posted multiple angles of the same rangoli, captions, different filters, anything to get noticed.

Boss kept liking random photos. No pattern. Just whenever he opened WhatsApp.

By month three, I was spending more time managing photo politics than actual engagement.

Boss finally called me.

"Why are the HRs so obsessed with posting photos?"

"Because you like them, Ravi."

"What?"

"You like the photos. They interpret that as approval. Now it's a competition."

Long pause. "I'm just acknowledging I saw it."

"They don't see it that way."

He stopped liking photos after that. Just viewed them.

The photo race cooled down. Slightly.

Half my time went to managing who posted what, when, and why the boss didn't react.

The actual employees? Nobody asked if the activities mattered.

Somewhere in that WhatsApp group, three blurry rangoli photos are still waiting for someone to appreciate them.

Good Ideas Travel. Credit Doesn't.

Delhi. Large retail chain. Five thousand employees spread across India.

Problem: New processes rolled out. Nobody reading SOPs.

Digital access limited. Physical manuals gathering dust.

I had an idea.

Regional offices print short FAQs. Put them on notice boards.

Add incentive: quiz based on the content.

Winners get recognized, small rewards.

Simple. Low-cost. Effective.

It worked.

Employees participated. Managers noticed.

General Managers sent thank-you emails.

Head Office appreciated the initiative.

Years later, a colleague pulled me aside.

"You know the Regional Head wasn't happy about that quiz thing, right?"

I blinked. "Why?"

"Country Head called her. Asked why she hadn't thought it earlier."

Pause.

"She got pulled up because of your initiative."

I stared. "But... it helped the employees. It worked."

"Doesn't matter. You made her look bad.'

The initiative succeeded.

The organization benefited.

But the Regional Head got questioned.

I never apologized.

Didn't even know I was supposed to.

Good ideas travel fast in corporate life.

Credit doesn't.

Midnight Updates, Morning Backstab

My manager went on long leave. Personal reasons.

I didn't ask. He didn't offer details.

In his absence, I ran the restaurant.

No disasters. No escalations. Tables turned. Guests left fed. Staff showed up. Cash tallied.

Then the calls began.

Late nights. 10 PM. 11 PM. Sometimes midnight.

First week, I thought it was normal.

Second week, I realised it wasn't concern. It was surveillance.

"Covers?"

"Full house."

"Walk-ins?"

"Yes."

"Bar sales?"

"On target."

"Any problem?"

"None, sir."

The questions never changed. Only the time did.

One night, 11:47 PM.

"Everything okay?"

"Yes, sir. Last table just left. Closing in ten minutes."

"Good. Call me if anything comes up."

Nothing ever did.

Three weeks later, he returned.

Next day, I was called to his boss's cabin.

He was already there.

Numbers. Feedback. Upcoming weekends.

Then the boss turned to me.

"Will you be able to handle the restaurant if needed?"

I said, "Sir, I've been running it for three weeks…"

He cut me off.

"Your manager feels you're not ready."

I looked at my manager.

He didn't meet my eyes.

"Sir," I said, "I've been updating him every night. Covers, sales, service flow."

The boss nodded.

"I know. That's why I'm asking you."

Silence.

"There were no complaints," I added.

"That's precisely why we're having this conversation."

We were dismissed.

Outside, my manager caught up.

"I didn't mean it like that…"

"You called me at midnight for three weeks," I said.

"Then told your boss I can't handle it."

He muttered something about not taking chances.

Four months later, I was transferred to another outlet.

The Resignation That Hurt Feelings

Some bosses treat resignations like exit formalities.

Some treat them like break-ups.

This GM? Third category.

The day one of his direct reportees resigned, you'd think someone had questioned his lineage, leadership, and lunch choices, all at once.

First reaction: disbelief.

Second: silence.

Not the peaceful kind. The weaponized kind.

Emails stopped. Meetings vanished. Eye contact? Cancelled.

The guy was still coming to office every day, serving notice period like a good employee, but being treated like a ghost who hadn't died properly.

Then came the Last Days Special Package.

Suddenly, all the work that hadn't moved for months became urgent.

Deadlines appeared from nowhere.

Reviews scheduled at 4:45 PM.

Files returned with comments like "Revisit" and "Think again", no explanation.

Less notice period, more emotional punishment.

Midway through his notice period, I tried saying something, lightly.

"He's anyway leaving," I said. "No point stretching things now."

He didn't react. Just nodded.

That nod people give when they've already decided to feel hurt.

Later that day, while discussing something else entirely, he said quietly:

"After all I did for him…"

By the last week, the silence returned.

No farewell.

No handshake.

No "all the best."

Just a chair that became empty one evening, and nobody mentioned it again.

As if the person had never existed.

Some people don't get fired.

They get emotionally deleted.

The GM moved on to his next hire like nothing happened.

Until the next resignation.

Section C: You vs The System

The Barcode Swap

When Your Reportee Reports to Someone Else

The Guy Who Deleted Everything

SECTION C: You vs The System

The Barcode Swap

Four well-dressed women spent far too long examining mixer grinders.

Saturday afternoon. Peak hours. Store packed.

They walked straight to home appliances. Mid-30s. Shopping bags already in hand.

We had three ranges:

Budget (₹2,500), mid-range (₹4,500), top-end (₹7,500).

They handled every display piece. Opened boxes. Checked inside. Read manuals.

Too slow. Too deliberate. Too much interest in the boxes themselves.

One floor staff member whispered to security,

"Keep an eye on that group."

Finally, they picked two mixers and headed to billing.

Cashier scanned them.

Two budget models. ₹2,500 each.

Total: ₹5,000.

They paid. Smiling. Giggling. Walked toward the exit.

Security stopped them for a routine check.

Opened the first box.

Top-end mixer. ₹7,500 model.

Second box. Same.

Invoice: two budget models.

Boxes: two premium ones.

Security called me over.

"These aren't the models you paid for."

Immediate outrage.

"We didn't do anything!"

"Your staff packed this."

"This is your mistake."

One woman got louder. "Train your people properly. How is this our fault?"

I asked security to pull footage from home appliances. Last hour.

Five minutes later, he showed me the video on his phone.

Clear enough.

They'd moved to a corner they clearly thought wasn't covered.

Opened boxes.

Swapped products.

Resealed them.

Carried the wrong boxes to billing.

I showed them the clip.

Silence.

Then one last attempt:

"We were just checking quality. Maybe we got confused."

"You put a ₹7,500 mixer in a ₹2,500 box. By accident?"

No answer.

"You can either pay the difference now, or we call the police."

They paid the extra ₹10,000. No apology. Just muttered complaints as they left.

Later, the security guard said, "Sir, this happens every weekend. Different faces. Same trick."

"How often do they get away with it?"

"If we don't catch them at the exit? Every time."

I looked at the door. One guard. Too many customers. Too many bags.

That night, we added another security guard. Increased bag checks.

Didn't stop it.

Just forced them to get smarter.

When Your Reportee Reports to Someone Else

I had a Store HR reporting to me. On paper.

In reality, my boss called her directly. Training programs.

Meetings. "Quick help." "Just five minutes."

Nobody told me. Not my boss. Not my reportee.

At first, I thought it was a one-off. Then it became routine.

Work started slipping.

She was doing two jobs. Mine officially. His unofficially.

Then came the WhatsApp statuses.

"Best manager."

"Best mentor."

"So grateful."

Not about me.

Fair enough. I was apparently just the person CC'd on her career.

Then things went wrong.

Some complaint reached the MD.

Suddenly, the boss who'd been bypassing me remembered reporting lines existed.

That's when I was remembered.

"Can you document all the lapses?"

"Call your reportee."

"Ask her to meet me."

When the work was being assigned directly, I wasn't in the loop.

But when things caught fire, I was handed the extinguisher… with my name on it.

My reportee sensed the shift. Started calling for guidance.

I gave it. Not because I was noble. Because she was stuck between two bosses who couldn't figure out their own mess.

Then came the final instruction.

"Issue a show-cause notice. CC me."

I wasn't managing. I was documenting the exit.

She resigned two weeks later.

Official reason: personal reasons.

The Guy Who Deleted Everything

Large retail chain. Mid-career.

Ashish reported to me.

First six months, solid.

Then things started slipping. Missed deadlines. Soft excuses.

I tried once. Then twice.

"Ashish, what's going on?"

"Sir, family issues. I'll improve."

He didn't.

Then right-sizing happened.

Corporate language for layoffs.

My boss called me in.

"We need to let someone go from your team."

We both knew who.

I called Ashish.

"The company's restructuring. Your role is being eliminated."

Silence.

"You'll get one month. Come in. Apply for jobs. Take interview leave. I'll support where I can."

He nodded.

"Okay, sir."

That month, he showed up. Quiet. Professional.

Applied everywhere. Nothing worked.

End of the month, he came back.

"Sir, I haven't found anything yet."

I went to my boss.

He sighed. "One more month. That's all."

Ashish didn't celebrate.

He just nodded again.

Second month looked the same.

Work. Interviews. Rejections.

End of month two.

"Sir, still nothing."

"We can't extend anymore. Friday will be your last day."

He accepted it. No argument.

That final week, he did a clean handover.

Detailed emails. Folder paths. Everything mapped.

"Project files here. Reports there. All organised."

I remember thinking: He's handling this well.

Friday came. Cake. Handshakes. Awkward wishes.

He left.

Two weeks later, my boss asked for a report.

Six months old. Ashish's work.

"It'll be in his folder."

It wasn't.

Nothing was.

IT checked.

"Sir… properly deleted. Cleanup software. No backup."

That's when it hit me.

The neat handover. The calm exit. The politeness.

The work had already been erased.

We rebuilt what we could. Some things were gone forever.

Ashish never responded.

He'd moved on. New job. New city.

Good for him.

The handover had been perfect.

Too perfect.

Chapter 6: How Things Actually Work

The Conman Who Said He Was Secret Service

The Overripe Papaya

The 200ml Coconut

The Offer That Disappeared Between Two Bosses

The Gift That Got Returned

The Resignation That Never Happened

The Budget That Never Happened

CHAPTER 6

HOW THINGS ACTUALLY WORK

The Conman Who Said He Was Secret Service

Second hotel job. New city. I'm 23, trying to make an impression.

Every morning at breakfast, there's this gentleman. Mid-40s, well-dressed, charming.

We'd chat while he ate. He told stories about his work, government intelligence agency. Classified stuff. Foreign missions.

I was impressed. At 23, who wouldn't be? Guy seemed like he'd walked out of a spy movie.

He'd drop names.

"Met with so-and-so last week."

"Working on a sensitive case."

"Can't talk about it, but big developments coming."

I believed every word.

Then one week, he stopped coming for breakfast.

Didn't think much of it.

Two weeks later, I'm at the desk. Phone rings.

"Good morning, Coffee Shop, how may I help you?"

"Crime Branch. Are you the manager who handles the restaurant?"

My heart stopped.

"Yes."

"Report to our office tomorrow morning. 10 AM."

"What is this regarding?"

"We'll discuss tomorrow."

He hung up.

I stood there holding the phone, brain racing. Crime Branch?

What did I do?

What could I have possibly done?

That night, I didn't sleep.

Went through every interaction, every guest. Nothing.

Next morning, I called in sick. Took a taxi to the Crime Branch office.

Stern officers. Buzzing fans. People waiting nervously.

An officer called me into a room. Pointed at a photo.

"Have you seen this man?"

I looked. It was him.

The breakfast guy. The intelligence agent.

"Yes. He used to come to our hotel for breakfast quite often."

The officer nodded.

"What did he tell you about himself?"

"He said he worked for some government intelligence agency. Classified work. Missions."

The officer almost smiled. "He's a conman."

I stared.

"He targets hotels. Befriends staff and guests. Claims to work for Intelligence. Gains trust. Then borrows money. Uses hotel staff names to build credibility with victims. By the time people realize, he's gone."

"How much did he take?"

"From various people? In lakhs. We've been tracking him for months."

I felt like an idiot. "I believed everything he said."

"You're not the first. That's why he's good at it."

The officer pulled out his visiting card. "If he contacts you again… calls, shows up, anything…inform us immediately."

I signed something. Left.

Walked out of that office feeling like I'd aged five years.

For weeks after, every time a charming guest started telling impressive stories, I'd think: is this another conman?

Never saw him again.

Don't know if they caught him.

Breakfast went back to being just breakfast.

The Overripe Papaya

Room service. I was the manager.

I had a captain working the opposite shift, I did mornings starting at 6 AM, he handled evenings and nights.

One morning, routine shift. Took handover, signed the register, walked the floors checking for overnight trays.

Everything looked normal.

Then the VP stormed into the room service department.

Face red. Shouting. Throwing things, clipboards, files, papers, onto the floor.

I'd never seen him like this. The VP was usually calm, composed, soft-spoken.

Now he was yelling.

"Who was on duty last night?" "Who served Room 303?"

He spotted me.

"You. My office. Now."

Inside his cabin, the sales manager was already there, standing quietly in the corner.

"Do you know who the guest in Room 303 is?" he asked.

"No, sir. I just started my shift. I wasn't here last night."

"He's an airline captain. Handles crew accommodation contracts. Year-long contracts. Entire airline crew."

I nodded.

"He's put in a complaint."

I waited for the rest, food poisoning, misconduct, something serious.

"He says he's moving the entire crew contract to another hotel."

That landed.

"What was the complaint, sir?"

"The papaya boat served to him early morning was overripe."

I looked at him, not sure I'd heard correctly.

"Overripe," he repeated. "Papaya."

The sales manager jumped in. "Do you know how much effort it takes to secure a client like this? Revenue loss. Reputation damage."

I tried explaining. "Sir, this happened on the previous shift. I wasn't here. The night captain was on duty…"

"You're the manager," the VP said. "You're responsible. I don't care which shift it was."

I said nothing after that.

"Call the night captain. Get him here."

This was before mobile phones. Landlines. I was expected to track him down at home and summon him in the middle of the day, on his off hours, for a papaya.

"I'm considering suspension," the VP added.

Suspension. Over a papaya.

He dismissed me with instructions.

"Fix this. Apologise. Do whatever it takes to retain the contract."

Two days later, pieces started coming together.

Someone mentioned the airline had been talking to another hotel. Better rates. Extra perks. Airport transfers.

The captain had been staying with us for months. No issues. No complaints.

Then suddenly, this.

By the time the papaya appeared, the contract already seemed... unsettled.

The complaint made everything official. Gave it a reason. Something neat to put on paper.

Nobody apologised to me. Nobody said maybe we overreacted.

The VP never brought it up again. The sales manager moved on to the next emergency.

The papaya wasn't the problem.

But I was the manager on duty when the complaint landed.

So I became it.

The 200ml Coconut

Retail chain. Handling fresh food delivery for premium clients.

One of them: elite golf club. High-end members. Very particular.

They ordered fresh produce. Including green coconuts.

Orders going fine for months. On time, good quality.

Then: complaint.

I called the club manager.

"What's wrong?"

"Coconut water. The quantity's inconsistent."

"It's fresh produce. That happens."

"They sit together at breakfast after their rounds. CEOs. MDs. Staff cuts the coconuts tableside. Pours the water into glasses."

Pause.

"If one person gets less than another, they notice. They compare. The one with less complains."

CEOs comparing coconut water at breakfast.

"Serve them whole," I said. "With straws. Nobody would know."

"Not our service standard. We cut tableside."

"Then you're showing them the difference."

"Can you source uniform coconuts?"

"No. They grow on trees."

Long silence.

"If you can't guarantee consistency, we'll reconsider the order."

We lost the account.

Six months later, their competitor club signed up. Same coconuts. Same variance.

They served them whole. With straws.

Nobody complained.

The Offer That Disappeared Between Two Bosses

Final round interview. Big retail chain.

Both of them in the room together. Ms. A and Mr. B.

A proper interview. Questions, answers, discussion. It runs long.

* * *

They split up after the main interview.

Ms. A comes in alone.

"We have a Regional HR Manager role. Six stores. Reports to me. Based in Gurgaon. Interested?"

"Yes."

"Good. I'll recommend you."

She leaves.

* * *

Mr. B walks in next.

"I've been looking at your profile. You'd be better as Zonal Training Head. Twelve stores. Multiple regions. Reports to me. Interested?"

"I'm open."

"Let me discuss with the team."

He leaves.

* * *

Ms. A returns. She closes the door.

"What did he offer you?"

"A zonal training role. Reporting to him."

Her face changes.

"That role isn't confirmed. Mine is approved. Budget, headcount, everything. Tell him you want my role."

"But he said…"

"If you push for his role, you'll end up with nothing."

She walks out.

* * *

Mr. B comes back in.

"Have you thought about the training role?"

"I'm open. I can work with either."

He pauses.

"We're looking for someone to build the training function. If that's not what you want, we don't need to proceed."

"I'm comfortable with what you think fits."

He nods.

"We'll get back to you."

He leaves.

* * *

Nothing happens after that.

Two weeks pass. No call.

I follow up with the recruiter.

"Ms. A left the company last week."

Pause.

"They're reviewing the role structure."

A month later:

"They've decided to go with an internal candidate."

The Gift That Got Returned

Retail chain. My boss managed field teams across cities.

One of them, Manoj, hated reporting to him. Turf war thing. Sales ego. The usual.

We'd send small gifts for birthdays. T-shirt, coffee mug, whatever.

Manoj's birthday. He's stationed in some other city. My boss orders a company t-shirt, couriers it to his hotel.

Boss tells me: "Sent Manoj a birthday gift. Thought it'd be nice."

"Cool."

Week later, courier shows up. My boss opens it at his desk. I'm sitting right there.

It's the t-shirt. Sent back.

With a note.

Boss reads it. Face goes red. Hands it to me.

The note: a lecture about knowing your customer. About not making assumptions. About basic sales fundamentals.

Ending: "Know your customer before you send gifts."

Sales 101. Delivered as an insult.

I look at the t-shirt. "What size did you send?"

"Large. My size."

"What size is Manoj?"

Pause. "Should be Large."

Manoj's XL. Maybe bigger.

"So he sent it back?"

"With a lecture."

Boss wanted to call him.

"Don't," I said. "He's already pissed."

Boss didn't call. Kept the t-shirt in his drawer. Would pull it out sometimes and stare at it.

Tension lasted weeks. Every call awkward. Every email stiff.

Eventually it faded. Not because they resolved it. Work just kept moving.

Then Manoj got transferred. Different department. Different city.

Nobody sent him a t-shirt when he left.

Weeks of tension. Over a Large that should've been XL.

The Resignation That Never Happened

Hotel days. Different hotel. Different manager.

One morning he calls an urgent meeting. All restaurant managers.

Urgent meetings usually meant someone screwed up and we were about to be grilled.

We gathered. Bracing.

But this time, different.

He started talking about how the GM had "wronged" him. Full emotional saga. Building sympathy.

Then he dropped it:

"I have decided to quit."

The room froze.

Silence.

The kind where everyone looks serious but internally is celebrating.

Because let's be honest… 99% of us were thinking: "Hitler se chhutkaara finally."

Except his one chamcha. That guy looked genuinely worried.

The manager looked around. "What do you all think?"

Nobody wanted to answer. But survival instincts kicked in.

"Sir, you must not leave."

"Sir, forgive him. Managers come and go."

"Sir, the department will collapse without you."

"Sir, if you go, we will also quit."

His chest was swelling. He was feeling the love.

Then from the corner of the room, one guy spoke up:

"Sir, you should definitely quit. GM has been unfair with you."

The room froze again.

Manager's face went red.

He realised instantly: this wasn't support, this guy actually means it.

Without another word, he waved us off.

Meeting over.

He never mentioned resigning again.

The Budget That Never Happened

Hotel days.

The pub had old-world charm. Dark wood, low lights, familiar regulars.

It had worked for years.

But time does what it does. Quietly. Without permission

Wear and tear crept in quietly. Upholstery faded. Fixtures aged. The music system worked, but sounded tired. Meanwhile, competition around us was reinventing itself. New pubs. Better lighting. Sharper sound.

Customers still came.

They just asked the same question now and then:

"So… when are you renovating?"

For six months, we pushed for a revamp.

Management finally agreed to hear proposals.

Three departments: F&B, housekeeping, maintenance.

We worked 24 hours straight. Numbers, vendor quotes, cross-department coordination. Everything updated till the last minute.

D-day. Shower at the hotel. Suit up. 9 AM sharp.

My turn.

I walked them through the pub revamp.

"Total investment: ₹8.5 lakhs. Expected ROI: 18 months, driven by increased footfall and premium pricing."

The MD nodded. Asked questions.

The CFO asked about payment terms. I explained.

They huddled.

Twenty minutes later, we were called back in.

"All three proposals are approved. F&B, housekeeping, maintenance. Congratulations."

We walked out exhausted. Elated.

Finally, the pub would evolve without losing its soul.

Weeks passed.

Then months.

Nothing moved.

Vendors kept calling.

"When do we start?"

"I don't know. Waiting for final approval."

"But you said it was approved?"

"It was. We're waiting for… implementation clearance."

I didn't even know what that meant.

I asked the CFO.

"Sir, when are we starting the pub revamp?"

"Soon. Finalizing the timeline."

Two months later:

"We're reviewing cash flow. Budget's tight."

Next quarter:

"Let's revisit after the festival season."

Festival season came and went.

I stopped asking.

One evening, the CEO did his rounds.

He stopped in the pub. Looked around.

"Place needs a revamp," he said casually.

I looked at him.

"Sir, we presented a revamp proposal eight months ago. It was approved."

He smiled.

“Approval doesn’t mean implementation.”

I blinked.

“We approved it. Didn’t say when.”

And he walked away.

We had worked 24 hours for a presentation that meant nothing.

The pub ran on the same aging charm, year after year, till I left.

Two years later, a colleague told me:

“They renovated the pub.”

Everything we had proposed.

After I was gone.

PART THREE

THE PERSONAL COST

Chapter 7: When Plans Meet Reality

The Leave That Wasn't

The Appraisal Bell Curve

The Whistleblower:he Guy Who Found the Fake Invoices

The Price War We Couldn't Win

Second Day, Grabbed by the Collar

When the Person Firing You Gets Fired First

CHAPTER 7

WHEN PLANS MEET REALITY

The Leave That Wasn't

I took three days off. First break in seven months.

Plan: visit parents in Kolkata. Spend time. No laptop. No work calls.

Day one went fine. Flight. Home. Dinner with family. Phone stayed quiet.

Day two, morning, 9:30 AM. Phone rang. Manager.

"Where are you?"

"On leave, sir. Till Thursday."

"Oh. Right. Listen, can you quickly check something?"

I should've said no. I said, "What's the issue?"

"Payroll escalation. Finance is saying the salary breakup has errors. Need you to verify. By noon."

I opened my laptop. Parents watching TV in the next room.

Checked the file. No error. Format was different from what finance expected. That's all.

Called payroll. "Resend with revised format. It's fine."

Done. Closed laptop.

11 AM. Another call. "Just need five minutes."

Twenty minutes later, still on call.

1 PM. Email marked urgent.

3 PM. WhatsApp. "Quick question."

By evening, I'd worked four hours. On leave.

Parents asked, "You're on holiday?"

"Yes."

But laptop was open. Phone was buzzing.

Next day, manager called again.

"Thanks for yesterday. One more thing…"

I took the call.

Later, my father asked, "Do they know you're on leave?"

"Yes. He approved it. Two months back."

"Then why are they calling?"

Nothing had been urgent before I applied for leave. Files were fine. Deadlines were manageable.

The moment I wasn't physically in office, suddenly everything needed me. Immediately.

I came back after three days.

Manager said, "Hope you had a good break."

I nodded.

Three days off. Twelve hours worked.

That wasn't leave. That was remote work with guilt.

Next time I took leave, I told them I was going to a remote area. Very poor network. Almost no signal.

And I stopped answering calls after 10 AM.

They managed. Somehow.

Turns out urgent wasn't as urgent as they thought.

The Appraisal Bell Curve

At the retail chain, appraisals were a nightmare.

Management insisted on fitting everyone into a bell curve. Top 10% get the highest rating. Bottom 10% get the lowest. Everyone else in the middle.

On paper, it sounded neat.

I had a team of twelve. Two were genuinely stellar. One was struggling. The rest did their jobs, showed up, caused no trouble.

The curve didn't care.

Only one person could get the top rating. One person had to take the bottom.

So I picked one stellar performer for the top slot. The other got the second-tier rating. Not because she didn't deserve it. Because the slot was already used.

The struggling guy got the bottom rating. Even though he'd improved a lot over the year. He wasn't failing anymore. He was just the weakest.

He quit three weeks later.

The other stellar performer quit too. Three months after that.

In his exit interview, he said, "I worked my ass off and got the same rating as people who just showed up. What's the point?"

I mentioned the bell curve.

He wasn't interested. "I don't care about curves. I care that my work wasn't recognized."

He was right.

The curve didn't change. Neither did the exits.

The Whistleblower: The Guy Who Found the Fake Invoices

Different company. Reputed retail chain. I'm in operations, handling vendor payments.

Accounts guy, Akshay. Quiet. The type who checks numbers three times before sending anything.

One day he comes to my desk.

"Sir, there's a mismatch. ₹3.2 lakhs."

"Data entry error?"

"I checked. Three times. It's not an error."

He showed me. Payments made to a vendor code that didn't exist in our system.

I took it to my boss.

Boss looked at it. "I'll handle it."

Two weeks later, nothing happened.

Akshay wasn't satisfied. Sent an email to the finance head. Copied audit. Detailed breakdown of discrepancies.

Next day: meeting. Finance head, internal auditor, his manager.

They thanked him for his diligence. Assured him it would be investigated.

Week later: Akshay got moved to a "special project." Data cleanup. No team. No deadlines. Just busy work.

His cabin shifted to a corner near the storeroom.

System access revoked. "For security purposes."

Three months later, the person linked to those vendor codes was transferred to another region. Redesignated.

A year later: Zonal Finance Head.

Akshay's appraisal: "Meets expectations. Needs to focus on assigned tasks rather than areas outside his scope."

He quit six months later. Small company. Back-office role.

The Price War We Couldn't Win

Competitor opening next door. Big chain. Deep pockets. Grand opening banners everywhere.

Head Office panicked.

Late evening, I'm doing closing checks. Phone rings. Category Manager from HO.

"Price revision coming."

"How many products?"

"Most of them. List coming by 11 PM."

I looked around the store. Thousands of SKUs. Shelf labels on every product.

"How many people for the night shift?"

"Two people. That's what's budgeted."

At 11 PM, the email landed. Excel sheet. 3,000+ revised prices.

Subject line: "URGENT – Implement before store opens 6 AM."

I did the math. 3,000 labels. Two people. Nine hours.

That's 333 labels per hour. About six labels per minute. Non-stop. No breaks.

Physically impossible.

But the email didn't ask if it was possible.

It just said "Implement."

We started. Printed labels in batches. Replaced them aisle by aisle. Groceries first. Personal care. Whatever we could reach.

At 3 AM, someone asked, "Chai?"

We walked to the dhaba across the street. Ordered chai. Nobody talked. Just drank and went back.

By 7:30 AM, we'd done maybe 2,000 labels. Still over a thousand products with old prices.

Store opened.

Within an hour:

"This rice is cheaper next door."

"Your cooking oil is ₹10 more."

Not everything. Just enough.

By afternoon, footfall was down.

That evening, the phone rang again.

Category Manager: "We reviewed today's numbers. Some categories are still off. Another revision tonight."

Their teams had done fresh competition benchmarking, some by visiting the store as customers, some through contacts who knew what prices were coming next.

Same Excel nightmare. Same two people. Same impossible deadline.

Second revision the next evening. Third revision two days later.

We kept going back. Kept changing labels.

Customers kept going next door.

The competitor's opening lasted two weeks. Our night shifts lasted a month.

Second Day, Grabbed by the Collar

Second day. First job. Five-star hotel.

Someone grabs me by the collar.

Middle-aged guy. Not in uniform. Not smiling.

"Don't come tomorrow."

He let go. Walked away.

I stood there thinking: Excellent. Two days in and I'm already getting fired by someone who doesn't even work in my department.

Went to the Personnel Manager. This was before "HR." Just Personnel Manager. Old-school.

"Sir, someone just threatened me."

He barely looked up. "Who?"

"I don't know. Some guy. Grabbed my collar. Said don't come tomorrow."

"I'll handle it."

"But…"

"I said I'll handle it."

Great. So reassuring.

Next day, I came back. Nervous.

Ten minutes in, same guy appeared.

"You came?"

"Personnel Manager said…"

"Tang todke raste mein fenk dunga."

(I'll break your legs and throw you on the street).

I was twenty years old. New city. Didn't know anyone.

I went home. Didn't go back.

A week later, Personnel Manager called. "Can you come meet me?"

He had a new offer letter.

"We've resolved it. Different designation. Management Trainee instead of Operations Trainee. Same salary. The issue is... that guy? Union leader. Political connections. They wanted the Operations Trainee position for their people. We've moved you to a non-union category."

I wanted to say: So you just let a goon threaten a 20-year-old till he stopped coming, then shuffled some papers to make it go away?

But I needed the job.

So I took the letter.

Worked there for two years. Saw that guy in the corridors regularly.

Never spoke. Never crossed paths.

He could've ended my career on day two. He knew it. I knew it.

Worked there two years. Left. He's probably still there

When the Person Firing You Gets Fired First

Ex-colleague called one evening.

"My boss called me today. He says, look out for a job.

Three months. He'll confirm next week."

"Get it in writing," I said. "Ask for dates."

Next week, he went to the boss's cabin.

Boss didn't look up.

"I'll call you. I'm in the middle of something important."

He didn't call.

Days passed. No email. No follow-up. No clarity.

My colleague called again. More nervous now.

"What if after two months they say, we already told you?

Then I'll have only one month left."

He was right to worry.

So he started looking. Quietly. Desperately.

Problem was, his CTC was 15 lakhs.

Too expensive for mid-level roles.

Too junior for senior ones.

Rejections came fast. Some polite. Some silent.

Weeks passed.

About a month later, he called again.

"You won't believe this."

I waited.

"The boss who was supposed to sack me…"

"…quit."

Pause.

"Yesterday was his last working day."

That was it. No warning. No announcement. Just gone.

My colleague was still there. Same desk. Same access card. Same job.

The three months vanished. The threat expired. The calendar reset.

He laughed. Not relief. Something else.

"I wasted one month," he said.

I didn't know what to say.

Next appraisal cycle, his reporting manager changed.

The three-month warning? Never mentioned again.

Corporate has no memory.

Only anxiety does.

PART FOUR

SURVIVAL AND REBUILDING

Chapter 8: Still in the Circus

The Meeting Went Well

The Receptionist Who Became Head of Technology

Meerut, Summer Heat

The Night the Fax Machine Resigned Before the Staff Did

The HRMS Interview That Ended Mid-Screen

The Kaneydda Dream

CHAPTER 8

STILL IN THE CIRCUS

Twenty years in.

Thirty years in.

The stories don't stop.

The absurdity doesn't end.

You just get better at recognising it.

The Meeting Went Well

Early hotel days.

I was told to go meet a guest. Some work. Some discussion. Don't remember what.

I remember this part very clearly though.

Took my scooter. Vespa.

Did the meeting. Whatever it was, it went well.

On the way back, it started drizzling.

That Kolkata drizzle. Enough to make roads shiny. Not enough to make you careful.

There was a bus in front of me. Another bus behind me.

The one in front slowed. I decided to overtake.

At the same time, the bus decided to accelerate.

I couldn't slow down. Behind me was another bus. Slowing down meant getting sandwiched.

Bus drivers don't believe in personal space. Or brakes.

So I went for it. Overtook. Cut left.

And then…tram line.

The scooter slid. Boom.

I don't know if I blacked out or time just skipped.

Next thing I remember…noise. People shouting. Tyres screeching.

I opened my eyes. Everything was black.

My first thought: *Achha. Dead.*

Then I realised…it wasn't darkness. It was a bus tyre.

A few centimetres from my face.

I rolled away. Limped to the side.

Didn't check myself. Didn't check the scooter.

Passengers were reacting. Some abusing. Some sympathetic.

One gentleman picked up my Vespa, parked it properly, and handed me the keys.

Didn't say anything. Just nodded.

I gathered myself. Kick-started the scooter.

The handle was bent. I straightened it by force.

Good enough.

Went back to the hotel. Changed my torn uniform. Back on duty.

Boss saw me.

"How was the meeting?"

"Good, sir."

Only later at home did I notice the scratches. The blood.

Never told family. Never told office.

The Receptionist Who Became Head of Technology

Twenty-eight confirmation letters.

Probation completion. Six months done. Boss approved. Send the letters.

Between three client calls and five escalations.

Due by 6 PM.

Open template.

Update name.

Update designation.

Update date.

Save. Send. Repeat.

By 5:47 PM, done.

Sent the last one. Closed the laptop.

At 6:02 PM, the first email arrived.

Thank you for sharing the confirmation letter.

I noticed the designation mentioned does not match my offer letter.

My correct designation is VP – Technology, whereas the letter states Director – Technology.

Could you please update and resend the corrected version?

I opened the attachment I'd sent him.

Wrong designation.

Then another email.

My job title is listed as Director – Technology.

It should be Associate AI.

Please check.

Thank you,

Pranav A

I opened my Sent folder.

Started checking.

The receptionist's letter said *Head of Technology.*

The actual tech head's letter said *Office Support Assistant.*

One junior hire had become *VP – Strategy.*

Some had start dates from last year.

Twenty-eight letters sent.

Fifteen people now correcting me.

Phone kept buzzing.

Polite emails. Screenshots.

“No urgency, just flagging.”

I drafted one response.

Sent it to everyone who'd written in.

Thank you for bringing this to our notice.

There was a versioning issue during document processing.

Please find the revised letter attached and kindly disregard the earlier version.

By 8 PM, corrections sent.

Nobody escalated.

The receptionist who'd been briefly promoted to Head of Technology didn't mention it again.

Neither did I.

Meerut, Summer Heat

New store opening in Meerut. Peak summer. Peak recruitment drive.

My interview room: One fan. Two stools. One rickety table. No AC. No water cooler nearby. Just heat and candidates trying not to faint.

By 11 AM, the room felt hostile. I was sweating through my shirt. People waiting outside looked cooked.

Seventh candidate walked in. Young woman. Early twenties. Simple kurta. File in hand.

We started. Basics. Experience. Availability.

Five minutes in, I noticed she was pale. Not nervous. Drained.

"You okay?" I asked.

"Yes, sir."

"You want water?"

She hesitated. "I'm fasting, sir."

"Vrat?"

She nodded.

"In this heat?"

"Yes, sir."

I pushed my bottle across anyway. "Drink it. In case."

She smiled politely. Didn't touch it.

We continued. Two questions later, her voice slowed. Then stopped.

I looked up.

She wasn't looking at me anymore.

"Hey…are you okay?"

No answer.

She swayed.

Then collapsed.

We got help. Moved her out. Water. Shade. Fan straight on her.

After a few minutes, she came around. Mortified.

"Sir, I didn't eat. And today's vrat… and the heat…"

"It's fine," I said. "Do you want sees a Doactor?"

"No, sir. I'm okay."

I rescheduled her interview. Two days later. Early morning.

She came back. Same kurta. Clear eyes. Answered everything cleanly.

We hired her.

A few months later, I visited the store. She was on the floor, handling customers, managing stock.

Saw me. Came over.

"Sir, you remember my interview?"

I nodded.

"Next time," she said, "breakfast first."

I laughed.

She went back to work.

Store opened two weeks later. The interview room was gone.

Next NSO: different city, same heat, same one-fan setup.

The Night the Fax Machine Resigned Before the Staff Did

One night, after shutting down my restaurant, I noticed the business centre lights still on.

I went in to check my mail. The computer began its prehistoric 1990s warmup. Then I heard a sound:

Tringgg... szzzz... thap! szzzz... thap!

The fax machine suddenly woke up like it had taken personal offence to my presence.

Resignation letter. Another one. And another. Five total.

These weren't random resignations. These were the hotel's blue-eyed MT-turned-Managers, the chosen ones.

One of them was my restaurant chef.

My first thought: Sabotage. Coup. Mutiny. Or maybe the fax machine finally snapped.

Should I inform someone? Should I pretend I didn't see anything? Should I take the papers and run?

I decided to do what every sensible hospitality professional does during chaos: I walked out quietly.

Let HR earn their salary.

The next morning, I entered expecting alarms, HR panic attacks, and at least three emergency meetings.

But no. Nothing. Business as usual.

Only the air was tight, the kind of silence where everyone knows something but no one wants to be the first to say it.

My chef said he was "not feeling well."

A week later the news broke... all five had quit.

And the best part? They opened a restaurant together.

Today it's a big chain across India.

The HRMS Interview That Ended Mid-Screen

Post-COVID. Between the fashion startup collapse and finding consulting work.

Consultant fixes an interview. HR role at a mid-sized company. Decent opportunity.

Interview day, I log on. Lady interviewer appears. All smiles. Polite.

We're chatting about my experience. She's asking about my HR background, what systems I've worked with, what projects I've handled.

Then she asks, "Have you ever launched a new HRMS from scratch? Full implementation?"

"I've worked with HRMS…payroll, attendance, performance management. But a complete launch from scratch? No. I've been part of…"

She cuts me off.

"Thank you."

Pause.

Then: "We'll get back to you."

Screen goes blank.

One criterion. I didn't meet it.

She hung up mid-sentence. Mine, not hers.

The Kaneydda Dream

Training session. Retail chain. Freshers. Fresh out of Class 12. First jobs.

Most of them weren't taking it seriously. Showing up late. Half-hearted effort.

So I gave them the motivational talk.

"You're young. You have potential. Work hard, and you can grow here. We had a security guard who became a Department Manager."

I paused for effect.

"So tell me. What do you want to do in life? What's your objective?"

I was expecting: "Sir, I want to become a manager." "Sir, I want to grow in retail."

First kid: "Sir, Kaneydda jana hai."

Second kid: "Sir, Kaneydda settle hona hai."

Third kid: "Sir, mujhe bhi Kaneydda."

I looked around the room. Ninety-five percent of them: Kaneydda.

I stood there thinking: I'm lecturing them about growing in retail, and their entire plan is to escape to Canada.

Made sense.

I tried pivoting. "Okay. Canada. Fine. But you need experience first. Work here two years, build your resume, then apply."

A few nodded. Most looked like they were already Googling visa consultants.

One kid stayed back.

"Sir, realistically, what are my chances?"

"Of going to Canada?"

"Yes."

"Tough. Expensive. Long process."

"But some make it, no?"

"Some do."

He looked determined. "I'll try anyway."

"Good luck."

Six months later, he quit. Better pay elsewhere.

Two years after that, LinkedIn message. Profile picture: snow-covered landscape.

"Sir, I made it to Canada. Working in a warehouse. Pay is decent."

I replied: "Congratulations."

Another kid from that batch messaged a year later. "Sir, I applied for Canada four times. Rejected every time. Trying to settle here now."

After that training session, I stopped asking freshers about their long-term plans.

* * *

Part Four started with small absurdities, wrong emails, fainting candidates, dreams of Canada. Those felt manageable.

What came next wasn't

* * *

Chapter 9: When Everything Collapsed

The Call I'll Never Forget

When the Salaries Stopped

Pink Slips

The Great Corporate Weight Loss Program

The Replacement I Recommended

The Pub Years: When Friendships Had Expiry Dates

The One-Fifth Salary Job

When My Body Also Gave Up

The Client Who Wanted 110%... Until Sunday

CHAPTER 9

WHEN EVERYTHING COLLAPSED

The Call I'll Never Forget

Different retail company. Well-established. Reputed brand.

I was neck-deep in a project when I got the call. My mother had a stroke.

Called my manager. No response. Texted: "Mother serious, need leave, please approve."

Rushed to the hospital.

She texted back late evening: "How is your mother?"

I replied: "Still serious. In coma. Under observation for 48 hours."

I lost her within those 48 hours.

After the rituals, I joined office. Still processing. The loss. The emptiness.

That day, my boss called me for a meeting. List of pending work. Then:

"Arup, you know what helps with grief? Throwing yourself into work. Just drown yourself in it."

I came out of the cabin. Sat at my desk. Stared at the laptop.

Excel therapy. For bereavement.

I finished the project. Met the deadline. Got a "good job" email.

Three months later, I quit.

Last week of notice period. Handover done. Exit formalities complete.

She called me to her cabin.

"We need you to extend. Two more weeks. Just until we find a replacement."

I looked at her.

"If I was critical to the role, this should've been planned earlier. There should've been a backup."

She started to say something.

"I've completed my handover. Everything's documented. If you need anything after I leave, I can help over phone."

"But…"

"I'm leaving as per my notice period."

Silence.

"Okay."

I walked out.

When the Salaries Stopped

Fashion startup.

COVID hit. Lockdowns. Empty stores. Sales tanked.

Salaries stopped.

First month:

"Cash flow issue. Coming next week."

Second month:

"Investors pulling out. Hold tight."

Third month:

Phones stopped ringing.

Different employee. Different crisis.

11:30 PM. My phone rang.

Sobbing voice.

"Sir, my father needs surgery. I need ₹50,000. I was counting on this month's salary."

Half-asleep, trying to respond properly.

"I don't have any update on salaries…"

"Sir, please. Can the company give me an advance? Surgery is on Monday."

I emailed finance.

Emailed the promoters.

No response.

Next morning, I called her back.

"I tried. Nobody's responding. I'm sorry."

Long pause.

Then: "It's okay, sir. Thank you for trying."

She quit two weeks later. Found another job.

I don't know what happened to her father.

The promoters stopped answering calls.

Phones switched off.

The CFO tried holding things together.

"Promoters are working on funding. Salaries will come soon."

Then:

"They're in talks with investors."

Then his tone changed.

"I don't know, Arup. They're not telling me anything either."

"You're the CFO."

"I know. But every time I ask, they say 'we'll discuss later.' Then they disappear."

A few weeks later, the CFO didn't show up.

I called him.

"You okay?"

"I quit. Can't do this anymore. I'm not going to lie to employees for people who won't answer my calls."

He found another job within a month.

Six employees came to office.

Sales team. Hired just before COVID.

Two months in, salaries stopped.

They sat across from me.

No shouting. No threats.

Just waiting.

One said, "Sir, it's been two months. I have rent. EMIs.Hope you understand"

Another asked, "Have you spoken to the founder?"

I had.

I told them what he said.

"Aapko rakha hai. Aap handle karo."

The sentence just sat there.

One of them asked, very calmly,

"Then what are we supposed to do?"

I looked at them. Then said something I hadn't told anyone yet.

"I haven't been paid either. Five months."

The room went quiet.

"You also…?"

"Yes."

Working.

Living off savings.

One asked, "Then why are you still here?"

"Same reason you kept coming. Hoping they'll pay."

Silence.

Eventually, the promoters paid.

In parts. Over months.

After enough people had already left.

I left soon after.

Pink Slips

New MD joined. Decided to cut an entire layer of middle management. All stores. Same day.

Severance package. Notice pay. Lists prepared.

Ambulances arranged. Security briefed.

Atmosphere was gloomy. People scared.

I was at the regional office when it happened. We had a team deployed to each store. HR rep, operations rep, security nearby just in case things got physical.

My phone started ringing at 9 AM. Store 1.

"Sir, we've started. First person just got the letter."

"How'd they react?"

"Crying. Asking why. We explained it's business restructuring. They're not taking it well."

Second call, 9:30 AM. Store 3.

"Sir, one person fainted. We've called medical."

"Serious?"

"No, sir. Panic attack. We're giving them water, letting them calm down."

By noon, most stores were done. But the calls kept coming.

The hardest call came from Store 7.

The HR rep was crying.

"Sir, I can't do this anymore. These people have families. Kids. One guy's daughter is getting married next month."

"I know. But the decision's been made. Just finish the process."

"Sir, this doesn't feel right."

"It isn't."

She hung up. Finished the layoffs. Quit two weeks later.

People were called, one by one. Some cried. Some fainted. Some got angry. Some refused to accept.

Disbelief. Trust broken after working for so many years.

After that, if an HR walked inside the store with papers, employees would say:

"Aaj kiska number hai?"

The Great Corporate Weight Loss Program

The day the pink slips came, almost an entire middle layer across stores disappeared.

Department managers, assistant managers, supervisors…gone in 24 hours.

We thought: Bas. Rightsizing done. Company's lean now.

The new staffing structure was tight. Each store had bare minimum people. One guy responsible for the floor. One guy for billing & admin. One guy to do everything else. And three guys to pray the store doesn't catch fire.

But somehow, stores ran. Employees huffed, puffed, limped, but managed.

For a few weeks, things were quiet.

Then the new hires started arriving.

Not store staff. Not frontline hires.

Vice Presidents.

Associate Vice Presidents.

Deputy Vice Presidents.

Presidents of Nothing.

Directors of Something.

Heads of Who Knows What.

Strategy Chiefs.

Transformation Gurus.

One guy's designation was so long it needed two ID cards.

All with salaries so high the CFO probably needed therapy.

And the best part? Every single one of them was "close to the Top Man."

Some from previous companies, some from college, some from God knows where.

The same employees who were told "We must cut costs" were now whispering in washrooms:

"Cost kidhar cut ho raha hai, bhai? Store mein ya spreadsheet mein?"

They fired the people who did the work.

Then they hired people who supervise PowerPoint.

People who supervise meetings about meetings.

Employees would whisper: "Sir, hum log kam hain. Kaam zyada hai."

The VP count reached 14 by month three.

The Replacement I Recommended

Bengaluru. Head Office. One of my teammates got a great offer. Better money. Better title.

She left. We wished her well.

Six months later, my phone rang. It was her.

"I'm not happy there. Culture's terrible. Role isn't what they promised. I want to come back."

She'd already called my boss. He hadn't responded. So she called me.

"Can you put in a word?"

I did.

Spoke to my boss. "She wants to return. Good worker. We could use her."

He didn't say much. Just nodded.

Week later, she called again. "Any update?"

I spoke to him again. Suggested a specific role. Made the case.

He thought about it.

Then one day: "Ask her to call me."

Approvals taken. Dates fixed. She came back.

Settled in. Worked well. Everything normal.

Then restructuring happened.

My boss called me in. "Someone needs to go to Punjab."

"Okay. Who?"

"You."

I stared at him. "Why me?"

"You're not from Bangalore. She is. Local person. Makes sense to keep her here."

I was doing well. Built systems. Trained people.

But I wasn't local.

So I had to go.

The person taking over my responsibilities? Her.

The colleague I'd pushed to bring back.

I handed over everything. Files. Contacts. Projects I'd started.

She thanked me politely. Moved into my role.

I moved to Punjab.

She sent me a LinkedIn request three months later.

I accepted it.

The Pub Years: When Friendships Had Expiry Dates

5 Star hotel, I ran one of Kolkata's most happening pubs.

I once told a newspaper:

"I don't see myself alive without being at the pub."

I believed it. The regulars, the crowd, the energy, it felt real.

Rich guys would call me every day to book liquor during happy hours. Discounted prices. They could afford full-price bottles, but loved bragging about the discount.

A few became friends.

Then I left. Moved to telecom.

The phone calls stopped. Suddenly. Completely.

I tried calling a couple of them. "Hey, want to catch up?"

"Busy, yaar. Some other time."

That "other time" never came.

Six months later, I passed by the same pub. New manager. Same crowd.

One of them saw me. Waved.

I waved back.

He went back to his drink. Didn't come over.

The One-Fifth Salary Job

I joined a role at one-fifth of my earlier salary.

Not "slightly less." Not "market correction."

One-fifth.

The offer email came. I read it twice. Refreshed my inbox. Checked if a page was missing.

Nope. That was the number.

I stared at the screen thinking: "So this is what rock bottom looks like. It has an offer letter."

What do you even negotiate at that point?

"Can you make it one-sixth?"

"Throw in a metro pass?"

I didn't argue. Didn't negotiate.

I just accepted it.

Every morning I showed up on time. Same laptop. Same work. Very different lifestyle.

Chai at office canteen instead of Starbucks.

Auto instead of Ola.

Monthly budget spreadsheet that made me cry.

Months later, someone at a meeting said,

"You must be expensive to hire."

I nodded. Sipped my chai. Changed the topic.

When My Body Also Gave Up

Post-COVID. The fashion startup had collapsed. I was jobless, sitting at home, trying to figure out my next move.

One morning, I noticed a small bulge in my lower abdomen.

Hernia.

Actually, two.

Because when life gives you problems, it never gives you one at a time.

The surgeon looked at me. “Single or double repair?”

I asked, “Can I do one now and one later?”

He shrugged. “Up to you. Pain is the same. Recovery is the same. If you can manage, do both.”

I said yes. Thought I’d save time.

Little did I know.

Closer to surgery day, the doctor suggested allergy tests. Blood test, whatever.

I was on the operating table, in the gown. Fully prepped. Monitors on. Assistants waiting. Feeling ridiculously exposed.

Then the doctor says:

“We cannot give you general anaesthesia. You’re allergic to half the chemicals we use.”

Great. Perfect timing.

Then: “We’ll inject your spine instead. But I cannot guarantee 100% success. Paralysis is a possibility.”

I just looked at him. Couldn’t think of anything to say.

But there I was, lying on the table, in a hospital gown, fully exposed, thinking: run? scream? negotiate? faint? None of it. I stayed. Partly because I was too frozen to move. Partly because… well, I was in a hospital gown. I don't know why I stayed.

***

No music. No drama. Just cold lights, cold steel.

The anaesthetist pricked my spine. Slowly, my lower body went numb.

Then the surgery began.

I couldn't feel pain, but I felt everything else.

The pressure. The pulling. The tugging. Something foreign being shoved inside, mesh being stuffed in.

And I was wide awake.

Listening to doctor's gossip, joke, teach some junior how to handle my intestines.

At one point, they laughed about something and I wanted to ask, "Guys, mujhe bhi sunao.. bore ho raha hoon!"

I was naked, half-paralysed, fully conscious.

***

The surgery finished. I didn't die. Or get paralysed.

So that was a win.

Then the painkillers wore off.

I couldn't breathe. Couldn't think. Just pain. Everywhere. Like someone was twisting a knife in my gut and wouldn't stop.

I cried. I begged. I questioned every decision.

They gave me painkillers strong enough to knock out an elephant, and still I felt everything.

But I survived the ICU night.

After two days, I went home…walking like a very old man.

Four weeks later, I was applying for jobs again.

The Client Who Wanted 110%... Until Sunday

During one of my startup stints, I met this young guy, Nikhil.

Full energy, full confidence, full speed. The kind who speaks like every sentence is a motivational quote.

Engineer. Ex-founder. Handled e-commerce with swagger.

He was fun to have around, a one-man energy drink.

Occasionally asked for guidance. Then he moved on, and life moved on.

Months later, while I was at home contemplating the next chapter of my life, my phone buzzed.

"Nikhil calling..."

He sounded stressed, overwhelmed, desperate - the holy trinity of startup existence.

"Arup, I really need your help. I want to improve. My company expects more. I know you can guide me. I'm ready to give my time, my effort... whatever it takes. I'll even pay you."

For a moment I thought: God is real. And He sends help through people who speak fast.

I agreed on one condition:

"You have to be consistent. Weekly calls. Dedication. No excuses."

He said, "Done, Arup. 200% committed. Please send the structure by weekend. I'll start Sunday."

I worked on the program. Spent time tailoring it for his personality. Sent it to him before the deadline.

And then...

Silence.

Complete Himalayan silence.

No reply. No message. Not even a "Seen."

I thought maybe he's busy, maybe the baby kept him awake, maybe he discovered a new mandi.

A month later, I received an email:

"Sorry, got busy... will start soon. Promise."

Then he ghosted again.

In startups, people often want transformation. But not as much as they want a Sunday nap.

EPILOGUE

WHERE ARE THEY NOW?

Priya (Salman Khan bathroom crisis)

Moved to another company eventually. We're still in touch. Still loves Salman Khan. Still denies she cried in the bathroom for thirty minutes.

The guy who said "ho Jayega" (Punjab store opening)

Works at another retail chain now. Store manager. Probably still saying "ho jayega," but now he makes it happen.

Rajesh (the guy who never got paid after the fashion startup collapsed)

Don't know. He stopped answering calls. Doubt he got his money.

Vikram (the colleague who stole my CV)

He got to the UK eventually. Moved abroad.

We spoke occasionally on Yahoo Messenger. Short messages. "How's work?"

"Good. You?"

That kind.

When he came back for his wedding, I attended. He seemed different. Quieter.

Then we lost touch.

One day, a common friend messaged: "Vikram died."

Mental health issues. Drinking. He'd collapsed suddenly.

I just remembered him asking me once if I wanted to apply to the UK too.

I'd said no.

Ravi (The Guy with Eight Dead Grandparents)

Outlasted three managers at the retail chain, including me. Still there. Family tree's probably stable now. Or maybe not.

The old-timer with the head twitch (Ice Bucket story)

Retired six months after that incident. Got his pension. Hopefully someone gave him a proper farewell, not just a plastic bucket.

The couple who eloped

Still married, far as I know. Both found jobs elsewhere. Made it work. Love won.

Akshay (found the fake invoices)

Works at a small trading company. Keeps his head down. Doesn't look for problems anymore. Can't blame him.

The founder who obsessed over fonts

Pivoted into a different line of business. Probably still checking Arial vs Calibri somewhere.

The trainee who said "May I light you?"

Became one of our best floor staff. Still tells that story at parties, apparently. Still alive, thankfully.

The guy who deleted everything before leaving

No idea. Never heard from him again. Hope karma caught up. Doubt it did.

CLOSING NOTE

If you've made it this far, thank you.

Some of you will close this book thinking,

"At least my workplace wasn't that bad."

Others will think,

"Wait. This is exactly my workplace."

And a few of you will think,

"Mine was worse."

You're probably right.

BEFORE YOU GO:

I've thrown in some bonus content ahead…quick absurdities that didn't fit the main chapters, survival glossaries for navigating Indian workplaces, and corporate buzzword translations.

Think of it as the chai break you deserve after surviving this book.

Still here? Still figuring it out?

Same.

Ho jayega.

Or it won't.

Either way, we'll deal with it tomorrow.

Arup Nag
January 2026

Bonus Content

Quick Hits: The Daily Absurdities

- LBDF – Looking Busy Doing F -all
- The Sleeping Salesman
- The Desk-Card Gang
- The HRMS Salary Glitch

Corporate Goodbyes

Survival Glossary

Corporate English Edition

Performance & People Management

BONUS CONTENT

The main book ends here.

What follows is the survival manual, the glossaries, the quick observations, and the languages nobody teaches you in onboarding.

For everyone who stayed till the end:

This is for you.

Quick Hits: The Daily Absurdities

These didn't fit the main narrative.

But they happened.

And they're too absurd not to include.

1. LBDF – Looking Busy Doing F -all

My first retail operations job taught me to spot a rare corporate species: LBDF.

Looking Busy Doing F-all.

There was this colleague. Every time I saw him, he was power-walking across the store like he was late for something critical. Frown on his face. Pen behind his ear. A stack of papers clutched to his chest.

Nobody had ever seen him sit. Or stop moving.

For weeks, I assumed he was the backbone of the operation - the guy holding everything together.

Then one day, I needed a file from his desk. He wasn't there. I looked through the papers he'd left behind.

Old printouts. Outdated circulars. A half-written memo from two months ago. Random stuff that had been sitting near the printer.

His "urgent documents" were props.

The man's entire job was momentum.

He'd cracked the ultimate corporate survival formula: walk fast enough with a serious enough face, and people will assume you're important and leave you alone.

Three months later, he got promoted.

Momentum pays.

2. The Sleeping Salesman

Startup days. Sales guy.

Every morning, sharp at 9:15, he'd show up, swipe in, and walk out with his laptop bag.

"Client meetings."

By 6 p.m., he'd be back, fresh, cheerful, ready to submit his daily reports.

Then audit checked his client logs. No meetings. No calls. Just perfectly filled reports and consistent claims.

He'd been going home. Sleeping through the afternoon. Returning in the evening to file updates.

When confronted, he smiled.

Audit later showed he hadn't done a single client visit that day.

We preferred employees who worked.

He was gone by the end of the week.

3. The Desk-Card Gang

Post-COVID startup. Small team. Access cards for attendance.

Sales team figured out a shortcut: cards left in a drawer.

Whoever reached early swiped for everyone else.

We caught it when six people clocked in at exactly the same time.

Every day.

CCTV confirmed: one person swiping multiple cards.

When we confronted them, the guy said: "Malum nahi tha, sir."

I raised an eyebrow.

"Kya pata nahi tha? Ki tum kisi aur ka attendance mark kar rahe ho?"

He looked down. "Sorry, sir. Galti ho gayi."

Warning letters went out.

Next week, everyone showed up on time.

Perfect attendance.

Then, slowly, the late marks started creeping back.

They'd learned to be less obvious.

4. The HRMS Salary Glitch

Retail chain. New HRMS update.

During onboarding, a deputy manager's salary got doubled.

Caught in verification. No payout. No damage.

But the ad-hoc HR operations head, who didn't understand the

System - wanted to issue a warning letter.

"You want to issue a warning letter for a system bug that none of us were informed about?"

"She made the error."

"The system made the error. She's used the same process for

six months. Hit Tab instead of Enter. New update bug."

Silence.

"Fine. No warning letter. But tell her to be more careful."

I told her later: "You're fine. No letter."

She almost cried. "Thank you, sir."

Corporate Goodbyes:

Out of Office, Out of Luck

Corporate India has a language for leaving.

Whether you're stepping away temporarily or being told you're no longer needed, there's always a script

Polite.

Professional.

Completely hollow.

When You Leave (Temporarily)

The "Out of Office" message became mandatory sometime in the early 2000s.

Before that, absence was simple. People waited. Or called your desk. Or gave up.

Now, absence needs documentation.

Explanation.

Justification.

Here's what I've collected:

The Overexplainer:

"Hi, thanks for the outreach. I am on PTO from 7th–12th March. Please factor in delays in my response. Appreciate your understanding."

Translation: I'm on leave but I'll still check email because boundaries don't exist.

The Minimalist:

"Out of office."

Translation: I don't owe you an explanation.

The Anxious Professional:

"Hi there, hope you are doing fine. I am out of the office with limited email access. For urgent matters, please text or call."

Translation: I'm on holiday but feel free to interrupt me.

The Honest One:

"Hi, I'm not feeling well and taking a day off today. Thanks, Hari"

Translation: I'm sick but I still logged in to set this message because that's what we do now.

Nobody's ever really "out of office" anymore.

We're on leave but checking email.

Sick but replying to urgent messages.

On holiday but "with limited connectivity."

The OOO message used to mean: I'm unavailable.

Now it means: I'm technically unavailable but will probably respond within 4 hours anyway.

When They Leave You (Permanently)

Then there are the emails where they're the ones leaving.

Leaving you behind.

Rejection emails.

Some arrive late. Some arrive final. All arrive carefully worded.

Version 1: The Late Apology

"Sorry for the late reply. We will not be able to take the candidature ahead. Thanks for the interest."

Translation: We forgot about you. Then remembered. Still no.

Version 2: The Vague Excuse

"Thank you for sharing the profile. Though it was liked, the client has some other expectations. Therefore, the candidature will not be taken forward."

Translation: "Liked" doesn't mean selected. "Other expectations" means we won't tell you why.

Version 3: The Volume Defense

"We received a large number of applications and, after careful review, regret to inform you that we will not be able to move ahead at this time."

Translation: You're one of many. That's supposed to make you feel better.

Version 4: The Diplomatic Mismatch

"After careful evaluation, we have concluded that our current opportunities will not effectively utilise your background and skills. We would be happy to stay in touch for future opportunities."

Translation: You're overqualified. Or underqualified. Wrong fit. We're not sure. Either way, no.

Version 5: The Post-Six-Rounds Special

"Based on the onsite discussion, we regret to inform you that the candidature will not be taken forward at this juncture. We wish you the very best."

Six rounds.

Online. Offline. Onsite discussions.

Multiple interviews. Time invested. Hope built.

Then: “Not at this juncture.”

Translation: We wasted your time. Here’s a corporate goodbye.

They all wished me the very best.

None of them meant it.

That’s corporate communication. Whether you’re leaving or being left, there’s always a script.

Professional.

Polite.

Perfectly hollow.

Survival Glossary

The Indian Workplace Dictionary You Didn’t Know You Needed

By the time you’ve worked long enough, you realize the language wasn’t casual. It was coping.

HO JAYEGA

They say: It will happen.

They mean: I have no idea how this will happen, I haven’t started, I’m already panicking, but saying “ho jayega” buys me time.

Example usage:

"Plan ready hai?"

"Ho jayega."

Reality check: It might. Or it won't. Either way, we'll figure it out later.

Believed by: Nobody. Not even the person saying it.

Corporate cousin: "It's on my radar."

BAS AA RAHA HOON 🚕

They say: I'm coming right now.

They mean: I haven't left yet..

Example usage:

"Where are you?"

"Bas aa raha hoon, sir. Five minutes."

Reality check: 45 minutes minimum.

Evolution:

→ "Bas nikal raha hoon" (still at home)

→ "Bas pahunch raha hoon" (still far)

→ "Bas parking mein hoon" (finally true)

JUGAAD 🔧

They say: Creative problem-solving.

They mean: Temporary fixes held together by hope, duct tape, and prayer.

Example usage:

"System crash ho gaya."

"Koi jugaad karo."

Reality check: The jugaad will work for exactly as long as you need it to. Plus five minutes.

Used by: Everyone who knows the proper solution is unaffordable.

DEKH LENGE 🤷

They say: We'll see / We'll figure it out.

They mean: We have no plan, no backup, no clue.

Example usage:

"Sir, target kaise achieve karenge?"

"Dekh lenge."

Reality check: Nobody's going to "dekh."

Cousin phrases:

→ "Kuch na kuch ho Jayega" (something or other will happen)

→ "Time pe soch lenge" (we'll think about it when the time comes)

AAJ NAHI TOH KAL 📅

They say: If not today, then tomorrow.

They mean: Stop asking.

Example usage:

"Payment kab ayega?"

"Aaj nahi toh kal."

Reality check: Neither aaj nor kal.

Finance department favourite.

ADJUST KAR LO 😤

They say: Please adjust / accommodate.

They mean: This is a mess, I can't fix it, and you're on your own.

Example usage:

"Sir, half the staff didn't show up."

"Adjust kar lo."

Reality check: Translation = "You're screwed, but suffer silently."

Common in: Retail, hospitality, events, festivals.

CHALEGA ✔

They say: It's acceptable.

They mean: This is substandard, definitely not what we wanted, but we've given up on excellence and this is close enough.

Example usage:

"Is this okay?"

"Chalega."

Quality levels:

→ International standard

→ Indian standard

→ Jugaad standard

→ Chalega ← You are here

Warning sign: If your boss says "chalega" about your work, something is wrong.

TENSION MAT LO 😰

They say: Don't worry.

They mean: You should absolutely worry, but I don't want to handle it.

Example usage:

"Deadline kal hai, kuch ready nahi."

"Tension mat lo."

Reality check: The calmer the tone, the worse the situation.

BOSS KA ORDER HAI 👔

They say: Boss has ordered this.

They mean: This makes no sense, but hierarchy demands obedience.

Example usage:

"Why are we doing this?"

"Boss ka order hai."

Reality check: Conversation over.

PERSONALLY DEKH LOONGA 👀

They say: I'll personally look into this.

They mean: I'll delegate it and forget about it.

Example usage:

"Urgent hai."

"Personally dekh loonga."

Reality check: Someone junior will handle it. Credit and blame will be reassigned later.

AAP HI SAMBHAL LO 🏃

They say: You handle it.

They mean: I've given up. You're on your own. Good luck.

Example usage:

"Sir, customer bahut angry hai."

"Aap hi sambhal lo."

Reality check: This is now your problem

Usually followed by: Manager suddenly unavailable

SAB THEEK HO JAYEGA 🙏

They say: Everything will be fine.

They mean: Nothing is fine, but optimism delays panic.

Example usage:

"Company collapse ho raha hai."

"Sab theek ho jayega."

Reality check: Hope buys time. Sometimes that's all you need.

Often said while: Updating resumes and calculating savings.

Corporate English Edition

For when Hindi is too honest and English is vague by design.

The Vague Ones

"Let's take this offline" 💬

They say: Let's discuss this separately.

They mean: I don't have an answer right now and don't want to look stupid.

Usually means: We're never discussing this again.

"Circle back" 🔄

They say: Let's return to this later.

They mean: I'm hoping you forget.

Translation: Never going to happen.

Timeline: 2-3 weeks before you give up asking.

"Action items" 📝

They say: Tasks to be completed.

They mean: Things discussed but rarely tracked.

Reality: 40% get done, 60% quietly die in someone's notebook.

"Quick win" 🎯

They say: Easy achievement.

They mean: Cosmetic improvement that looks good on slides.

Examples: Rebranding the cafeteria, new org chart that rearranges the same people.

The Polite Rejections

"Interesting perspective" 🤔

They say: That's an interesting point of view.

They mean: I disagree. Completely.

Polite variant: "That's one way to look at it"

"Let's think about it" 💭

They say: Let's consider this carefully.

They mean: No. Absolutely not.

Status: Forever pending.

"Noted" ✅

They say: I've acknowledged this.

They mean: I'm done listening. This conversation is over. Move on.

Tone decides whether it's neutral or quietly hostile.

"From a governance standpoint..." 📋

They say: Considering policy implications...

They mean: We're saying no safely. Blame it on policy/compliance/legal so nobody can argue.

Translation: "No – without debate."

"Let's be mindful of optics" 👁

They say: Let's consider how this looks.

They mean: It may be right, but it's politically inconvenient.

Reality: Optics routinely beat ethics.

The Buzzwords

"Synergy" ✨

They say: Combined effectiveness.

They mean: We don't have clarity, but this sounds strategic

Actual result: Two teams fighting over the same budget.

"Bandwidth"

They say: Available capacity.

They mean: I'm too busy (or don't want to do this).

Translation: "No, but make it about resources, not laziness."

"Best practice"

They say: Industry-standard approach.

They mean: Someone else did it first. We're copying them and calling it innovation.

Reality: It worked for them in different circumstances. May not work for us. We'll do it anyway.

"Moving forward"

They say: Going ahead / In the future.

They mean: Let's not talk about what just happened.

Used after: Any major screw-up that nobody wants to discuss.

***

Performance & People Management

"We need to manage expectations"

They say: Let's set realistic goals.

They mean: Lower them quietly, without saying so. Whatever was promised? Not happening. But we'll soften the blow gradually.

Translation: "Under promise what we already over-promised."

"High potential"

They say: Employee with growth prospects.

They mean: Works hard and complains less. Not necessarily talented -just compliant and willing to stay late.

Reality: Often means "does extra work for same salary."

"Culture fit"

They say: Aligns with company values.

They mean: Thinks too independently. We want someone who nods along, not someone who questions the system.

Reality: "Culture fit" = "Won't make us uncomfortable."

"Audit observation"

They say: Finding from review process.

They mean: Someone is in trouble. Papers will be shuffled. Emails will be sent. Nobody will be fired because hierarchy protects itself.

Outcome: Process changes that nobody follows.

If you've used more than five of these phrases in one meeting, you're either in middle management or you've given up entirely.

Possibly both.

ABOUT THE AUTHOR

Arup Nag has spent over 30 years working across hotels, telecom, retail, and startups in India, often arriving just as things were getting interesting.

He has built teams, handled crises, delivered bad news, and seen organisations unravel when money, patience, or accountability ran out.

Along the way, he learned that "ho jayega" is less a promise and more a survival strategy.

Sometimes it worked. Sometimes it didn't. The stories stayed.

This is his first book.